Thomas
Shabbou

ENCOUNTER SERIES

Law and the Ordering of Our Life Together

Essays by

Bruce C. Hafen
Thomas L. Shaffer
Susan S. Silbey
Richard Stith

and
The Story of an Encounter by
Edwin A. Rodriguez

Edited and with a Foreword by
Richard John Neuhaus

WILLIAM B. EERDMANS PUBLISHING COMPANY
GRAND RAPIDS, MICHIGAN

Copyright © 1989 by Wm. B. Eerdmans Publishing Co.
255 Jefferson Ave. S.E., Grand Rapids, Mich. 49503

Library of Congress Cataloging-in-Publication Data
Law and the ordering of our life together.

  Essays based on a conference sponsored by the
Rockford Institute Center on Religion & Society.
    1. Law and ethics—Congresses. 2. Law—Philosophy—
Congresses. 3. Religion and law—Congresses. 4. Chris-
tianity and law—Congresses.   I. Hafen, Bruce C.
II. Neuhaus, Richard John.   III. Center on Religion &
Society (New York, N.Y.)
BJ55.L37 1989   340'.11   89-11935
ISBN 0-8028-0211-7

Contents

Foreword

This is an ambitious book that comes out of an ambitious conference. Consider, for example, the exchange between Richard Stith and Robert Bork on whether every duty is accompanied by a right or whether there are some duties that are not attended by a right. That sounds frightfully esoteric but actually engages a question that is fundamental to our understanding of what the law is — and what the law should be.

Many Americans received their first real introduction to the philosophy of law during the five days of televised hearings dealing with the attempt to confirm Robert Bork to the Supreme Court in the fall of 1987. Passions surrounding Bork's nomination were, to say the least, intense; both supporting and opposing groups produced slogans at an astonishing rate. Indeed, many thoughtful observers believe that the intensity, even viciousness, of the attack on Robert Bork may have permanently changed the way this polity orders the relationship between the judiciary and the legislature. My own judgment is that the anti-intellectualism, bigotry, and vulgar distortions employed by Bork's opponents descended to a depth that is perhaps unparalleled in recent American public discourse. And yet, those who listened carefully to the hearings recognized that very basic questions were being joined about the meaning of law in America. What authority should be given precedent? Can we discern the "original intent" of the founders, and does it matter? How do we define the "core values" of the constitutional order? What is the connection between what is legal and what we, or the founders, deem to be morally "right"? Is there a "higher law" to which the law must always be subordinated and from which the law receives its "legitimacy"? In a democratic polity, how is the sovereignty of the people related to the authority of the constitutional text? Given the fevered partisanship of the hearings, these questions were seldom addressed directly or lucidly, but they were there nonetheless.

Disputes over such questions have been raging since the dawn of civilization, and they will continue, they *must* continue, so long as human beings believe that there is such a reality as justice. Aristotle said that the central question of politics is how we ought to order our lives together. From that, of course, comes the title of this book, "Law and the Ordering of Our Life Together." The word "ought" in Aristotle's formulation is the signal that these discussions and disputes are about morality.

In the earlier part of this century, many American jurists and students of the law scorned Aristotle's moral understanding of law in the "right ordering of the *polis*." In scorning Aristotle, they were also scorning Augustine, Aquinas, Maimonides, Calvin, Blackstone, and the writers and signers of the Constitution, among others. Those who sat in the seats of the scornful typically described themselves as, and were described as, "realists" or "positivists." They thought themselves very sophisticated, and in many ways they were. They had "seen through" moral pretensions about the law and come to the conclusion that the "majesty of the law" was, in largest part, a useful myth or noble lie. They believed that in fact the law was made up of laws, and laws were the product of interests, cultural biases, and other dynamics that had no claim to universal validity. This was a very adult and grown-up, if sometimes cynical, view of the law. To be fair, some positivists were not at all cynical. They thought they were simply being very modest and candid in saying that they could find no philosophical—never mind moral or theological—grounding for the law. But, whatever their motives, the proponents of realist and positivist views of the law led a generation or more to believe that the stated theme of this book and conference is an exercise in futility or, more likely, obfuscation.

At the same time, however, other legal scholars were calling for a fresh look at the connections between law, morality, and religion. One such scholar was Harold Berman, then of Harvard, who, as the reader will see, was a very active participant in this conference. Berman and others were instrumental in producing a new generation of scholars who have sharply — some think devastatingly—critiqued realist and positivist orthodoxies. Today there is a growing number of professional associations, meetings, and journals addressing the questions of religion and law. The leadership of this network of concern is well-represented in this book. They are not simply addressing religion-and-law questions as those questions come up in disputes over the religion clause of the First Amendment, with its free-exercise and no-establishment provisions. Those questions are very important, of course, and will become even more important as religion impinges more and more upon our public life. But behind those questions are the questions of moral truth, of philosophy, even of theology.

If we do not deal with the question of the law that is behind, above, and beneath the laws, we end up with the dismal proposition that "the law is the law is the law." That proposition is a certain formula for what social scientists call a "legitimation crisis" in the law. If there are no moral warrants, if there are no truths from which the law is derived, then more and more people will conclude that, in Dickens's memorable phrase, "the law is an ass." When, in a free and democratic society, enough people have reached that conclusion, all civil debate about how we ought to order our life together goes out the window.

While the renascence of interest in the connections between law, morality, and religion is mightily encouraging, we must not forget the sobering fact that it is still a minority, albeit a growing minority, that recognizes the urgency of attending to those connections. Some of the very best of that minority are represented in this book. When Robert Bork was asked by Senator Alan Simpson why he wanted to be on the Supreme Court, Bork said that one reason is that it would be "an intellectual feast." It may be too much to promise that you will find this book an intellectual feast, but I have no doubt that you will find it a very solid meal partaken in excellent company.

Many thanks to my colleagues Paul Stallsworth and Davida Goldman who, as always, labored long and successfully to make this conference work, and to Edwin Rodriguez, who did a heroic job of reconstructing the "story of an encounter" after his entire first draft went down the black hole of his word processor. We are especially grateful to the Pew Charitable Trusts, whose funding made this conference possible.

NEW YORK CITY   Richard John Neuhaus

A Sociological Interpretation of the Relationship between Law and Society

Susan S. Silbey

The announcement of this conference begins with the observation that although the "crisis in law" is perennial, it is nonetheless real and urgent. It is possible, the text continues, that "law itself has become morally lawless. That is, the connections between law and moral legitimations have increasingly been severed." In this essay I suggest that the problem should be more generally stated and that it is captured in the title of the conference itself, "Law and the Ordering of Our Life Together." What is in crisis and what is at stake in the perennial debate about the moral authority of law is the relationship between community and law; that relationship and the ways in which law contributes to the ordering of social life have constituted a principal focus of "law and society" research.

I begin by juxtaposing two visions of the relationship between law and society: the natural-law tradition and the sociological perspective. The sociological perspective describes law instrumentally. In this view, law makes available tools, resources, symbols, and languages useful in the construction of social order. In contrast, natural-law theories deny human agency a principal role for ordering social life and instead seek guidance and instruction in the morality of a universal, ahistorical "natural" law. After describing a sociologist's perspective on the relationship

1

between law and society, I will present a brief survey of what the sociology of law tells us about legal practices and how people use legal resources. Research from the sociology of law suggests that natural-law arguments are a form of idealism—perhaps a dangerous idealism, because they are unresponsive to and ignore the ways legal systems operate. I illustrate this with a propositional inventory of findings from the sociology-of-law tradition.

In section three, I offer a critique of the sociology of law suggesting that as the sociology of law exposes the idealism of the natural-law tradition, it may create in its own place a false or partial idealism. I try to characterize the "crisis in law" as it is expressed in this research tradition. I suggest that it has portrayed lawmakers as benign and law as relatively ineffective by focusing on state legality to the exclusion of law in its more pervasive and perhaps more salient dimensions. Finally, I urge attention to the role of scholars in contructing and deconstructing legality.

I

The history of this discussion has an ancient lineage, traceable from classical natural-law treatises to contemporary debates about literary and legal interpretation.[1] Two visions characterize the poles of this discourse.

The first vision understands law as a moral mirror reflecting ways of being, social relations, and conceptions of value and right the sources of which lie outside the law. In this vision, the distinction between law and society is less essential than the hierarchical relationship between law and moral values. For example, in its classical and modern incarnations, natural-law theory stipulates that there exists a set of universal, eternal, and immutable priniciples of social action and order that guide human interaction. These knowable patterns describe the preferred and essential character of human life. Although for some time it was

---

1. For a strong version of natural-right theories, see Leo Strauss, *Natural Right and History* (Chicago: University of Chicago Press, 1953). For an example of contemporary debates, see Ronald Dworkin, "Law as Interpretation," *Texas Law Review* 60 (1982): 527; and Stanley Fish's reply to Dworkin in "Interpretation Symposium," *Southern California Law Review* 58 (1985).

understood that natural justice was distinct from law and insufficient in and of itself for the governance of human societies, it eventually evolved into a standard by which to measure manmade law and to which positive law was accountable.

For example, Hadley Arkes's recent treatise on the relationship between morals and law is a contemporary attempt to locate the sources of law in a set of first principles. Citing both Aristotle and Kant, Arkes tries to show that particular moral and legal judgments on controversial questions of policy can be extracted from a set of first principles describing the human capacity for reason. It is possible to make judgments and oblige others to obedience, he argues, because the law is the collective embodiment of that human rational capacity. Following Kant, Arkes maintains that only a rational being could conceive the idea of law, a "moral rule which may be in conflict with his own self-interest." He further argues that law, which is the embodiment of collective social life, is necessitated by the existence of morals and "the nature of a being who [has] the capacity for morals."[2]

The alternative vision is distinctly modern. Premised on a separation between law and society, it emphasizes the problematic nature of an instrumental relationship between the two and views the relationship between morality and law as a version of the problematic relationship between law and society. This vision has roots in the political struggles of eighteenth-century Europe, a context in which a distinction between law and society was used to try to limit the power of the state.[3] Because the merger of law and society seemed an excuse for hierarchical oppression, liberal reformers tried to separate the two as part of an effort to end, or at least discipline, political control by the few. In the European context, law carries the historical burden of being part of hierarchy. For Americans, however, the rule of law was linked from the outset to the notion of the separation of law from state and society; matters of hierarchy and oppression were not significant issues. Instead, there is a persistent notion of external but neutral regulation and a conception of rationalized ordering. Law is viewed as something that has been produced by the state while

---

2. Arkes, *First Things* (Princeton: Princeton University Press, 1986), p. 8.

3. See John Locke's *Of Civil Government* (1690).

yet being able to control the state. This vision focuses less on the sources or morality of law than on its instrumental utility.

Out of the political upheavals of the eighteenth and nineteenth centuries and the social transformation we associate with the Enlightenment, there emerged a vision of an organic social order composed of an interactive web of contractual relationships. In response to a growing perception of the fragility of this social order and in an effort to shore up the sagging legitimacy of the European communities, which had been seriously shocked during a century of revolutionary transformation, scholars began to study, systematically and scientifically, the structures and processes of collective social life. The classical works of social science produced in the late nineteenth and early twentieth centuries gave a prominent place to analyses of legal phenomenon and the claims of various forms of legality.[4] During this century, scholarship produced in this tradition—under the various labels of sociological jurisprudence, American legal realism, and law and society research—has lent abundant support to the vision of an instrumental legal order.

Although the sociological tradition begins with ambivalence about locating morality in law, and thus emphasizes the law as a multipurpose device, it is nonetheless possible to read in the research a normative vision of legality. I will describe in thematic form some observations from the sociology of law before characterizing the moral vision of that sociology and what an alternative vision might look like.

II

The sociologist views law as a social institution, not something given in nature or deduced from first principles but rather created

---

4. See the following works by Max Weber: *Max Weber on Law in Economy and Society*, ed. Max Rheinstein (Cambridge: Harvard University Press, 1966); *Economy and Society: An Outline of Interpretive Sociology*, ed. G. Roth and C. Wittich (Totowa, N.J.: Bedminster Press, 1968); *Theory of Social and Economic Organization* (New York: Free Press, 1949). And see the following works by Emile Durkheim: *The Division of Labor in Society* (1893; New York: Free Press, 1964); *The Rules of Sociological Method* (1895; New York: Free Press, 1964); and *Professional Ethics and Civic Morals* (London: Routledge & Kegan Paul, 1957).

from patterns of human interaction. In this view, humans are the authors of all social arrangements, including law and the study of law; the social order and legality are "ongoing human production[s]."[5] Once constructed, however, a social institution takes on a life of its own, and becomes not only acted upon—that is, something in production—but something which acts upon its authors. It is perceived as external to humans, as an objective and controlling reality, something that is out there, that affects us and to which we respond. This controlling character, this ability to affect us, "is inherent in institutionalization as such": that is what we mean by the word *institution*. The control exists "prior to or apart from any mechanisms of sanction . . . [that may be] set up to support an institution" or define it, as in the case of law. The primary social control, or ability to regulate behavior, derives from the categories we routinely develop in interactions with others to typify and name events, persons, and things. Because these categories seem to exist independent of the persons who develop and use them, they are useful to the degree that they are shared. These typifications, by the very fact of their existence, control human conduct by identifying habituated "patterns of conduct, and . . . channel[ing] it in one direction rather than any of the many others that would be theoretically possible."[6] Through a dialectical process, humans produce a social world which they then experience as something other than human. Consequently, the institutional world thus produced "requires legitimation, that is, ways by which it can be 'explained' and justified" to each new generation that encounters it as made rather than in the making.[7] From this point of view, the law is a fundamental social institution, providing legitimations for the social order or stories that explain our lives to ourselves.

By setting forth the human invention of social institutions, the social constructivist perspective not only stands in marked contrast to natural-law theory but enables the empirical study of

---

5. The description of the sociological perspective in terms of socially constructed realities borrows from what has become the canonical formulation provided by Peter L. Berger and Thomas Luckmann in *The Social Construction of Reality: A Treatise in the Sociology of Knowledge* (Garden City, N.Y.: Doubleday, 1966), p. 49.

6. Berger and Luckmann, *The Social Construction of Reality*, p. 52.

7. Berger and Luckmann, *The Social Construction of Reality*, p. 58.

those institutions, including the sociological study of law. Reviewing the research from this perspective, I have generated at least six generalized observations about the ways in which people create and use legal resources. These observations describe law as an institutionalized mechanism for the use of authorized force in social groups. The ways in which this authority is used are situationally determined, characteristic of the organization of the task, and mobilized on the basis of socially constructed typifications. Although the uses and mobilization of law are situationally structured, it is possible to see cumulative consequences that reflect and reproduce larger social structural variables. This perspective describes law as a resource or tool for achieving an authoritative resolution of situations of discord or violence. It also suggests that we may expect too much from law, too much from rules. The following six observations are not mutually exclusive but collectively describe general features of legal behavior and institutions.

    1. *As both institution and practice, the law consists of historically and culturally developed activities regulating and legitimating the use of force in social groups.*[8] Although legal activity may rarely involve

------

8. Regarding the concept of law as both institution and practice, see Alasdair MacIntyre, *After Virtue* (Notre Dame, Ind.: University of Notre Dame Press, 1981). MacIntyre advances the concept of practice as a social activity "through which goods internal to that form of activity are realized in the course of trying to achieve . . . standards of excellence" that define and characterize the activity. At the same time, practices generally extend human ability. MacIntyre locates practices within institutions and also makes a point of distinguishing between the two: institutions serve specific interests and norms (external goods), he says, while practices are primarily concerned with internal goods. But he notes that it is possible to conceive of law both as institution and as practice. For a discussion of the appropriateness of the concept of practice for the sociology of law, see my "Ideals and Practices in the Study of Law," *Legal Studies Forum* 9 (1985): 7. For an extended, more critical and related discussion of praxis, see Richard J. Bernstein, *Beyond Objectivism and Relativity* (Philadelphia: University of Pennsylvania Press, 1985).

    The notion of law as regulation of the use of force in social groups should not be overstated so as to ignore resistance to law or its inability to regulate completely. Llewellyn's succinct description of law in *The Cheyenne Way* (Norman, Okla.: University of Oklahoma Press, 1941) begs that we recognize that "law exists also for the event of breach of law

the use of force, as Robert Cover puts it, the elaborate system of rules, decisions, and interpretations, and the activities associated with producing these nonetheless "takes place in a field of pain and death." In an article published in 1986, just after his death, Cover describes the relationship between legal practices and violence as follows:

> A judge articulates her understanding of a text, and as a result, somebody loses his freedom, his property, his children, even his life. Interpretations in law also constitute justifications for violence which has already occurred or which is about to occur. When interpreters have finished their work, they frequently leave behind victims whose lives have been torn apart by these organized, social practices of violence.[9]

Legal systems serve a range of functions in addition to regulating and legitimating force. These functions are often also performed by alternative institutions, however—often private associations; moreover, law is often redundant, exercising its

---

and has a major portion of its essence in the doing of something about such breach" (p. 20).

For discussions of the relationship between law and the use of force in social groups, see the works of Max Weber cited in note 4 herein; see also Oliver Wendell Holmes, *American Banana v. United Fruit Co.,* 213 U.S. 347, 356 (1908); and *Holmes Pollock Letters,* vol. 2 (Cambridge: Harvard University Press, 1941), p. 212. There is a rich literature distinguishing the concept of law as a body of rules *guaranteed by* force from the concept of law as a body of rules *about* force. See Karl Olivecrona, *Law as Fact* (London: Oxford University Press, 1959), p. 134; Hans Kelsen, *General Theory of Law and State* (Cambridge: Harvard University Press, 1949), pp. 25, 29; and Alf Ross, *On Law and Justice* (London: Steiner & Sons, 1958), p. 134. See also H. L. A. Hart's *The Concept of Law* (New York: Oxford University Press, 1976) for the view that force or coercion is a means for the realization of law rather than an essential feature of the concept of law itself. But if in fact law is not a body of rules guaranteed by force but a body of rules about force or rules that regulate coercion, as has been argued by Kelsen, Olivecrona, and Ross, a simplicity and elegance of formulation is achieved which seems to avoid recurrent problems of legal theory and raises the notion of law as the regulation of force to exalted status. A most concise and persuasive argument for law as a system of rules about force is found in Roberto Bobbio's "Law and Force," *The Monist* 48 (1965): 321-41.

9. Cover, "Violence and the Word," *Yale Law Journal* 95 (1986): 1601.

authority where it is inconsequential.[10] There is a great deal of interpenetration between private and public arenas in the formulation of law and the performance of such basic functions as resolving disputes and maintaining order, because those who regularly interact in valued long-term relationships usually form semiautonomous social fields, so that distinctions between public and private tend to disappear in practice.[11]

2. *In doing legal work, officials respond to particular situations and demands for service rather than general prescriptions or recipes of the task.* In this respect legal work is no different than other work: it is constituted by particular situations rather than general principles, and it proceeds on a case-by-case basis. This is certainly evident in the construction of law through litigation and the creation of precedent through decisions in individual cases;[12] it is also true in terms of law enforcement.

For example, police work is primarily reactive rather than proactive. With the exception of attempts to control sumptuary and so-called victimless crimes such as prostitution and drug dealing, police work begins with calls for help or citizen reports of crime or trouble.[13] Police do not patrol the streets with a vision of the criminal code in their minds, periodically checking to see whether the social scene is consistent with the requirements of law. Rather, police patrol with a vision of what is normal for this

---

10. See Patricia Ewick, "Redundant Regulation," *Law and Policy* 7 (1985): 421.

11. For a discussion of the basic functions and methods of law, see Lawrence Friedman, *The Legal System* (New York: Russell Sage Foundation, 1975).

Concerning the relationships that develop among those involved in the formulation and use of the law, see Sally Falk Moore, *Law as Process* (London: Routledge & Kegan Paul, 1978).

Concerning the distinctions between public and private arenas in this context, see Stewart Macaulay, "Law and the Behavioral Sciences: Is There Any There There?" *Law and Policy* 6 (1984): 145; and "Private Government," Disputes Processing Research Program Working Paper, 1983-86.

12. See, for example, Edward Levi, *An Introduction to Legal Reasoning* (Chicago: University of Chicago Press, 1961).

13. See Donald Black, "The Mobilization of Law," *Journal of Legal Studies* (1973): 125; and "The Social Organization of Arrest," *Stanford Law Review* 23 (1971): 1087.

neighborhood and respond to or intervene in situations, prompted by what they perceive to be unusual in this place or by calls for help signaling other definitions of the unusual. The police response to cases or calls is better characterized as handling the situation than as enforcing the law.[14]

This is also true in civil law enforcement and the regulation of business generally. Agents typically work on a case-by-case basis and create legal rules in response to particular demands for service. When coping with a never-ending flow of cases and when demands for service are a central part of law enforcement, case management becomes a critical skill of legal actors, often the defining characteristic of the work.[15]

Because legal action is situationally responsive rather than rule bound, it involves decisions and procedures of an extralegal nature. Legal actors operate with discretion. For example, the response to crime and the regulation of business by authorized officials involves decisions and procedures that are neither authorized nor described by law.[16] Faced with the decision of whether to arrest suspects in misdemeanor cases, police are influenced by the suspect's demeanor, deference, and responsiveness to their inquiries as much as or more than they are by the evidence that the suspect has violated the law.[17] In the mediation of family and juvenile disputes, court-appointed mediation agencies will not only provide a setting and process for consensual resolution

---

14. See Egon Bittner, *The Functions of the Police in Modern Society* (Washington: U.S. Government Printing Office, 1970); and "Police on Skid Row: A Study of Peacekeeping," *American Sociological Review* 32 (1967): 600.

15. In a study of the enforcement of consumer protection regulations in a state attorney general's office, I documented the processes by which case management produced substantive law. See Susan S. Silbey, "Case Processing: Consumer Protection in an Attorney General's Office," *Law and Society Review* 15 (1980-81): 849; see also Suzanne Weaver, *The Decision to Prosecute: Organization and Public Policy in the Antitrust Division* (Cambridge: MIT Press, 1977).

16. See Jerome Skolnick, *Justice without Trial* (New York: John Wiley, 1967); and my "Case Processing."

17. See Wayne LaFave, *Arrest: The Decision to Take a Suspect into Custody* (Boston: Little, Brown, 1965); and Irving Pilliavin and Scott Briar, "Police Encounters with Juveniles," *American Journal of Sociology* 70 (1964): 206.

of differences but will organize a range of therapies, provide ad hoc counseling, channel peripheral legal problems through other agencies, and become spokespersons for individuals and families with other official agencies, schools, and employers.[18]

The discretion that characterizes law work derives from conflicting mandates, resource constraints, and the inability to fully encapsulate experience in formulas or rules.[19] These restrictions create a need for space within the law for interpretation, innovation, and elaboration. Although statutes set theoretical limits to official action, they cannot determine how things are done within those limits. By choosing among courses of action and inaction, individual law enforcement officers become agents of clarification and elaboration of their own authorizing mandates.[20] They sometimes become moral entrepreneurs, not merely enforcing the rule but creating rules and extending their reach.[21] Bureaucrats become lawmakers, freely creating what H. Laurence Ross has referred to as a third aspect of law beyond written rules or courtroom practices.[22] This "law in action" arises in the course of applying formal rules of law in private settings and public bureaucracies; it is the interpretation or working out of authorizing norms through organizational settings.

3. *The characteristics of legal work inhere in the organization of the particular tasks, not the personalities of the actors.* For example, some hold that the police are socially divisive, that law enforcement is a tainted occupation, and that the police force tends to impose peremptory solutions on complex problems. But the

---

18. See Susan S. Silbey and Sally E. Merry, "The Problems Shape the Process: Interpreting Disputes in Mediation and Court," paper presented at the Law and Society Association Annual Meeting, 1987, and currently on file with the author.

19. See Kenneth Culp Davis, *Discretionary Justice* (Baton Rouge: Louisiana State University Press, 1969); and Mortimer H. Kadish and Sanford H. Kadish, *Discretion to Disobey* (Stanford: Stanford University Press, 1973).

20. See Kenneth Culp Davis, *Administrative Law Text* (St. Paul: West Publishing, 1972), p. 91; and Jeffrey Jowell, *Law and Bureaucracy: Administrative Discretion and the Limits of Legal Action* (New York: Duellen Press, 1975), p. 14.

21. See chapter 8 of Howard Becker's *The Outsiders* (New York: Free Press, 1963).

22. Ross, *Settled out of Court* (Chicago: Aldine, 1970).

problems being addressed by criticisms of this sort derive from
the nature of the task the police must perform rather than from
the individuals who constitute the police force.[23] Similarly, when
services are denied to handicapped children, it is more often a
result of the organization of schools than a reflection of the attitudes of teachers.[24] It is not for want of care alone that those in
need are not provided for; the recognition of need and the
responses available are shaped by organizational and cultural factors that incorporate and respond to, but are not determined by,
individual personality.

Along the same lines, the failure of regulatory agencies to
perform their mandated mission is more often a product of the
endlessness of the task and responsiveness of the agency than
dereliction of duty or malfeasance.[25] Agents in "street-level
bureaucracies" are expected to interact with clients regularly, but
their work environments are pressured and stressful.[26] Resources are limited, and mandates are too frequently ambiguous or
conflicting. The clients are the lifeblood of the organization, but
they are not the primary reference group for decision making.
As a result, it is difficult to assess and reward job performance.
Agents cope with these stresses by developing routines and
simplifications that economize on resources. They invent definitions of effectiveness that their procedures are able to meet.[27] In

---

23. See Egon Bittner, "Florence Nightingale in Pursuit of Willie
Sutton," in *Potential for Reform of Criminal Justice*, vol. 3: *Criminal Justice
Annals*, ed. H. Jacobs (New York: Russell Sage Foundation, 1974).

24. See Bonnie S. Hausmann, "Mandates without Money:
Negotiated Enforcement of Special Education Regulations" (Ph.D. diss.,
Brandeis University, 1985).

25. See my essay "Responsive Regulation," in *Regulatory Enforcement*, ed. Keith Hawkins and John Thomas (The Hague: Kluwer Nijoff,
1984).

26. Michael Lipsky coined the phrase "street-level bureaucracy"
to describe public offices serving clients' needs. Salient features of the
settings and characteristic coping mechanisms of public bureaucracies
apply to certain private agencies as well. See Lipsky, *Street-Level
Bureaucracy: Dilemmas of the Individual in Public Services* (New York: Basic
Books, 1980). See also Ross, *Settled out of Court*.

27. On this, see the President's Commission on Law Enforcement
and Administration of Justice, *Task Force Report: The Police* (Washington:
U.S. Government Printing Office, 1967), p. 15; Herman Goldstein,

so doing they may alter the concept of their job, redefine their clientele, and effectively displace the mandate of their organization and the law.[28]

4. *Legal actors respond to cases on the basis of typifications developed not from the criteria of law or policy but from the normal and recurrent features of situations.* These "folk" categories are used to typify the variation in an organization's workload and to signal appropriate responses, which are determined by the salient features of situations encapsulated by these categories. David Sudnow has described a public defender's understanding of the "normal" features of particular crimes in terms of the ways in which events "usually occur and the character of persons who commit them (as well as typical victims and typified scenes). . . . For example burglary is seen as involving regular violators, no weapons, low-priced items, little property damage, lower class establishments, largely Negro defendants, independent operators, and a non-professional orientation to the crime."[29]

Court personnel also make sense of and respond to cases through typifications of the relationships between the parties to a case.[30] Often these categories reflect the attention of the legal actors to the pacification of troubled situations rather than the identification and resolution of questions of interest or right, legal guilt or innocence. What the court refers to as a "barroom brawl" will have been a fight between strangers or acquaintances but not close friends. A "neighborhood" case will involve people who live in close proximity, although not necessarily in adjacent dwellings, and

---

"Police Discretion: The Ideal versus the Real," *Public Administration Review* 23 (1963): 140; LaFave, *Arrest,* pp. 102ff.; James G. March and Herbert Simon, *Organizations* (New York: John Wiley, 1958), p. 142; Victor Thompson, *Modern Organization* (New York: Alfred A. Knopf, 1961), pp. 14-15; Martin Shapiro, *The Supreme Court and Administrative Agencies* (New York: Free Press, 1968); Aaron Wildavsky, *The Politics of the Budgetary Process* (Boston: Little, Brown, 1964); Ira Sharkansky, *The Routines of Politics* (New York: Van Nostrand, Reinhold, 1970); and Thomas Anton, *Politics of State Expenditure in Illinois* (Urbana: University of Illinois Press, 1966).

28. See Robert Merton, "Bureaucratic Structure and Personality," *Social Forces* 18 (1940): 560.

29. Sudnow, "Normal Crimes," *Social Problems* 12 (1965): 255.

30. See Sally E. Merry and Susan S. Silbey, "The Problems Shape the Process."

it will often involve issues of space, noise, and children's behavior. A "friends" case may well involve people who live near one another, but the focus will not be the physical environment or children—although it may include a wider network of individuals, as is sometimes the case in neighborhood cases. Labeling an incident a "friends" case highlights the enveloping network of relationships that links the parties involved and draws others into the situation of conflict. A "barking dog" case is usually a neighborhood case that, as the label indicates, is regarded as relatively uncomplex, with limited ramifying relationships; moreover, this label indicates almost from the outset what the solution or outcome of the case will focus upon. A "girlfriend-boyfriend" case usually involves teenagers or other people living in their parent's household where parental disapproval of the emotional relationship between the couple is a major feature of the problem. In contrast, a "lovers" case typically refers to a more adult relationship, or at least one in which the parents of the principles are not involved.

There is a pointed reluctance among court personnel to stigmatize defendants by typifying them in criminal categories. Court staff believe that criminal records change relationships, and they are reluctant to create those records. In the lower courts, one rarely finds a case discussed or typified in terms of its legal designation, and if a case is talked about in legal categories, the implication is quite unambiguous: this is a serious matter. Much of the court's work falls into a very general category—"garbage"— which is used to distinguish minor interpersonal disputes from serious crimes, the latter being crimes that involve personal injury or costly property damage or use of a gun.[31] The general typification and sorting of cases as serious or garbage pervades case-processing organizations; it is not limited to courts.[32]

5. *The legal system reflects and reproduces the encompassing so-*

---

31. For a discussion of what constitutes a serious case, see Malcolm Feeley's discussion of what a case is worth in the lower courts in *The Process Is the Punishment* (New York: Russell Sage Foundation, 1979). For a discussion of case worth in a distinctly different setting, see Stanton Wheeler, Austin Sarat, and Kenneth Mann's *Sentencing White Collar Offenders* (New Haven: Yale University Press, 1988).

32. See Claire Larracey Lang, "Good Cases, Bad Cases: Client Selection and Professional Prerogative in a Community Mental Health Center," *Urban Life* (1981): 289.

cial structure.[33] Law is costly, and the costs are distributed differentially according to social class, status, and organizational positions.[34] Whether in the eighteenth or twentieth century, rates of grievance and litigation reproduce patterns of class, ethnic, and gender stratification.[35] There are differential barriers not only to invoking law but also to complying with law and to passing along the costs of compliance to others. Sometimes legal regulation "operates as a kind of regressive taxation, burdening the have-nots far more than the haves."[36]

Although the uses of law may be situationally structured, the responses and behaviors of legal actors cumulate, with the result that they come to reflect a wider array of social forces than the facts of specific incidents. For example, the ways in which law is mobilized and made available by the police is shaped by the community beyond the enforcement agents, for example.[37] Similarly, federal law 94-142 was designed to provide public services for handicapped children, but it has been used to provide private education at public expense for middle-class children seeking personalized education.[38]

The mobilization of law reflects not only class differences but different norms and values as well. Research on the mediation of family and juvenile disputes suggests that the principal

---

33. See Marc Galanter, "Why the 'Haves' Come Out Ahead: Speculations on the Limits of Legal Change," *Law and Society Review* 9 (1974): 95; and "Afterword: Explaining Litigation," *Law and Society Review* 9 (1975): 347.

34. See Ewick, "Redundant Regulation."

35. See David Trubek, Joel Grossman, Bert Kritzer, William Felstiner, and Austin Sarat, *Civil Litigation Project Final Report*, Disputes Processing Research Project, 1983 (Madison: University of Wisconsin Law School); "Litigation in America," *UCLA Law Review* 31 (1983): 72; Richard C. Kagan, *Lawsuits and Litigants in Castille, 1500-1700* (Chapel Hill, N.C.: North Carolina University Press, 1981); and Leon Mayhew and Albert Reiss, Jr., "The Social Organization of Legal Contacts," *American Sociological Review* 34 (1966): 309.

36. Stewart Macaulay, "Law and the Behavioral Sciences," p. 152; and Galanter, "Why the 'Haves' Come Out Ahead."

37. See Donald Black, *The Behavior of Law* (New York: Academic Press, 1976); "Crime as Social Control," *American Sociological Review* 48 (1983): 34.

38. See Bonnie S. Hausmann, "Mandates without Money."

impact on family conflict lies not in its ability to resolve disputes but in its influence on habits of handling conflict.[39] Echoing Foucault's studies of medicine, asylums, and sexuality, researchers suggest that mediation provides a mechanism for distributing middle-class modes of interaction—discussion, negotiation, and bargaining—to groups in society who have typically handled conflict in different ways. Mediation appears to be a mechanism for inculcating process values rather than resolving particular conflicts.[40]

A study of victims of discrimination suggests that the costs of law extend to far more than just financial and class issues; indeed, law seems to come at the price of the ability to define and manage the presentation of self. In a study of individuals who had reported suffering some form of discrimination on the basis of age, sex, or race, Kristin Bumiller notes that her respondents refused to turn to law to redress their grievances because they wanted to avoid the tendency of the legal process to individualize grievances and to require them to speak through a professional, a lawyer.[41] Bumiller argues that these tendencies and requisites rob victims of a sense of being in control of their own lives and isolate them at a time when they are most in need of support. Her respondents claim a double victimization—first in becoming an "object of discrimination" and second in becoming "a case" in law. The capacity of the legal process to objectify individuals and situations—to construct them as examples of a general rule—is typically assumed to be a strength, but those who are objectified experience it as oppressive.

In an unrelated study of lower courts, I observed a similar phenomenon. Although defendants did not undergo social degradation (i.e., fall in public position or status) as had been predicted for courtroom interactions, they nevertheless experi-

---

39. See Sally E. Merry and Anne Marie Rochleau, *Mediation in Families* (Cambridge: Children and Family Services, 1985).

40. See Susan S. Silbey and Sally E. Merry, "Mediator Settlement Strategies," *Law and Policy* 8 (1986): 7; and *Politics of Informal Justice,* ed. Richard Abel, 2 vols. (New York: Academic Press, 1981-82).

41. See Bumiller, "Anti-Discrimination Law and the Enslavement of the Victim," Working Paper 1984-86, Disputes Processing Research Program, University of Wisconsin; and *The Civil Rights Society* (Baltimore: The Johns Hopkins University Press, 1988).

enced something unpleasant.[42] Most particularly, they experience the loss of control and autonomy—negative associations and impressions that seem to attach irrespective of outcomes of guilt or innocence.[43] Having to go through the process that involves what Erving Goffman might have called "personal defacement" seems to be the issue. Defense becomes the assertion of self, an attempt to deny the law's effort to distance the individual through mortification and stripping of the self and to construct the individual through an abstracted and formally orchestrated process.[44] Legal settings are unpleasant and humiliating because they are public encounters in which some participants lose their ability to manage the presentation of themselves.[45] This somewhat ironic observation suggests that defendants can lose their autonomy and privacy without necessarily losing their social status—because for the regular defendants and witnesses in lower court proceedings, privacy and autonomy are already lacking. The research provides support for notions of class that include access to and management of one's autonomy and privacy as defining variables.[46]

---

42. Harold Garkinkel has defined a degradation ceremony as "any communicative work between persons whereby the public identity of an actor is transformed into something looked on as lower in the local scheme of social types" ("Conditions of Successful Degradation Ceremonies," *American Journal of Sociology* 61 [1956]: 420); he has suggested that the effectiveness of status degradation devices will vary according to their situational organization and operation. He hypothesizes that courts might exercise a fair monopoly over status-degradation ceremonies because degradation has become an occupational routine.

43. See Feeley, *The Process Is the Punishment*.

44. See Goffman, *Stigma* (Englewood Cliffs, N.J.: Prentice Hall, 1963); *Interaction Ritual* (Chicago: Aldine, 1967).

45. For a provocative discussion of the management of presentations of self in legal settings, see Austin Sarat and William Felstiner, "Law and Strategy in a Divorce Lawyer's Office," *Law and Society Review* 20 (1986): 93.

46. Obviously, socioeconomic status affects one's ability to manage a balance of the public and private spheres (using these terms in their conventional, nontheorized form). Poverty, for example, leads to a lack of privacy in crowded and noisy living conditions; conversely, great wealth sometimes calls forth unusual public notice. The problems of poverty are exacerbated, however, when an individual tries to obtain help from public officials or agencies. The person must reveal informa-

The assertion that law and courts are mechanisms of social control is neither theoretically nor empirically surprising; neither is the assertion of a relationship between social control and social structure.[47] These assertions are interesting, however, in the face of repeated efforts to "reform" the law in the name of neutrality or objectivity—because the assumption of such objectivity would seem to be controverted by the law's status as a socially constructed phenomenon[48] and the fact that it serves as a multipurpose device.

6. *Law is a resource used by citizens and legal actors for handling situations and solving problems.* Law is a culturally variable phenomenon, and each society, culture, and subculture makes of it something that belongs to that grouping. With this observation,

---

tion about himself or herself to the clerks in the Social Security office, to social workers, to medical or school personnel. In local community courts, social workers, welfare officials, and school and court personnel are an integrated part of the lives of their clientele, some of whom are regular participants in court. Such individuals' ability to manage the presentation of self to others is severely limited, although they certainly develop strategies of adaptation and resistance. But in the end, those for whom the court experience is novel, those who are unconnected to legal institutions or other participants in the process, those without developed strategies of resistance, and in general players inexperienced in the ways of public agencies will be humiliated.

In a heterogeneous and complex society with little consensus on substantive values, privacy and autonomy may be better indicators of power and class than occupation or income. It is well understood that privacy is inextricably connected with power relationships, with the vertical organization of society: individuals and institutions with greater power force those with less power to divulge information. We know that variation in perception of courts is also related to class and occupation and may also be related to the ability to demand and control one's privacy. Much of the apparent class variation in the use and effect of the legal process, especially the criminal process, may also reflect the ability of some participants to control what is exposed and who has access to information about oneself. Because the lower classes enter the courts with relatively little of this autonomy, obviously the courts can remove relatively less of it from them. They are exposed in court, and they may be humiliated, but they do not see or experience social degradation to the extent that those who occupy higher social positions do.

47. On this, see Black, *The Behavior of Law.*

48. See Gary Peller, "The Metaphysics of American Law," *California Law Review* 73 (1985): 1152.

the sociology of law reveals the natural-law tradition to be a particular culturally developed vision or ideal; some may even view it as a pernicious ideal on the grounds that it denies other culturally developed ideals in the name of being the one natural and universal law.

The uses of law can be distinguished in terms of experienced and inexperienced users. Nonprofessional disputants turn to law to resolve situations that they are no longer able to resolve by themselves. Although the recourse to law can be regarded as a strategic move, one of several that are possible to resolve particular troubles, the mobilization of legal resources frequently requires overcoming normative constraints against such action, which is itself seen as a form of "making trouble." Any calculation of the utility of law or its alternatives has to take account of the cultural context and meanings attached to dispute-resolution mechanisms as well as the availability and efficiency of those devices.

In a study of the cultural context of disputing, I found that disputants prefer to handle interpersonal problems by themselves, through talk or avoidance.[49] Only when talk or avoidance fails do parties in conflict turn to an outside agency. So long as they seek a voluntary and congenial discussion with the other party, disputants feel that resorting to outside help and uninvolved parties is morally repugnant. When they are willing to turn to others for help with their problem, the parties no longer wish to settle their dispute by discussion and negotiation. At this point they no longer consider their problem a conflict of interest in which they have limited and negotiable goals; they have come to view it as a principled grievance for which they seek an authoritative and binding solution. It is in precisely those cases that have developed to the point where they seem unavoidable, incessant, and intractable that the grievance becomes principled and the grievant can justify going to an outside agency. When they reach this point, disputants often turn to law, seeking a third party to make a definitive and binding judgment about right and wrong. At this point, disputants want vindication, protection of their rights (as they perceive them),

---

49. The following discussion is based on research reported in Sally E. Merry and Susan S. Silbey, "What Do Plaintiffs Want? Reexamining the Concept of Dispute," *Justice System Journal* 9 (1984): 151ff.

an advocate to help in the battle, or a third party who will un-
cover the "truth" and declare the other party wrong. Observations
of legal processes suggest that courts rarely provide what the disputants are looking for, particularly to parties in complex interpersonal cases—but inexperienced plaintiffs do not know this.
They turn to law for an advocate and to get justice. They are frequently disappointed in situations that more experienced court
users can manipulate deftly.[50]

For experienced and professional legal actors, law provides
a multipurpose device for problem solving.[51] In litigation, police
work, defense, prosecution, and judgment, the outcome is frequently determined before an appropriate or applicable legal procedure is invoked.[52] For example, in the enforcement of consumer protection law, agents frequently invoke infractions of a
variety of other laws in the course of resolving consumer com-
plaints.[53] They have this flexibility because laws, in general, are
imperfectly enforced, and there is a likelihood that those whom
they are seeking to charge with violation of consumer protection
law will also be guilty of violation of such things as safety and
building codes, zoning or license rules, tax laws, and other infractions only remotely related to consumer protection, if at all.

Legal ambiguity, or at least the potential for ambiguity, is located not simply in language or abuse of law but in the domain
of legitimate use. Every provision of law, once set loose, is a can-
didate for all manner of uses. Laws have histories within which
their meaning and use change, often quite radically. The work of
legal historians provides rich illustrations. For example, Chambliss
has described how vagrancy laws changed from being a means of

---

50. See Sally E. Merry, "Going to Court," *Law and Society Review*
(1979): 891; and "Working Class Ideology and Law," *Legal Studies Forum*
9 (1985): 59.

51. For a discussion of the distinction between experienced and
inexperienced players, see Galanter, "Why the 'Haves' Come Out
Ahead."

52. For a discussion of the processes of legal reasoning and writ-
ing, see Karl Llewellyn, *The Bramble Bush* (Dobbs Ferry, N.Y.: Oceana
Press, 1969). In this collection of introductory lectures, Llewellyn urges
his law students to read cases as a post hoc justification of the decision,
not as a description of how that decision was made.

53. See Susan S. Silbey and E. Bittner, "The Availability of Law,"
Law and Policy Quarterly 4 (1982): 399-434.

securing a labor force in the fourteenth century after the Black Death decimated the English population to a means of controlling vagabonds and rogues engaged in criminal activities on the highways in the sixteenth century.[54] The action of replevin, devised in medieval England to protect agricultural leaseholders from landlords who detained their cattle, was resurrected in nineteenth-century Wisconsin by landlords to use against leaseholders engaged in lumbering.[55] And, as is well known, the imposing edifice of our federal drug control laws was erected on the foundation of a tax measure.[56]

This activity, whereby law becomes a tool that shapes social situations, feeds back upon the law so that the uses to which it is put eventually come to shape the content and substance of the tool, the law itself. It is a dialectical process in which the law is the raw material that legal actors create and work upon at the same time they use it to handle whatever matters demand.[57] The uses of law are not entirely predictable—but neither are they unlimited. While law is available for all sorts of uses, the ways in which it is put to use are constrained by sets of practices, conventions, ways of doing things within a society; in this culture those practices relate to courts, lawyers, litigation, claims of right, precedent, evidence, and judgment, not to ballet dancing, playing chess, marketing, or running for office.

In other words, while the law is more varied than a formalistic and mechanical view would have us believe, the variation is neither indeterminate nor completely determined by external variables. Law is not only a set of doctrines; neither is politics the only reality. The way law is practiced, or what is done in the name of law, is constrained by a world of its own creation,

---

54. William J. Chambliss, "A Sociological Analysis of the Law of Vagrancy," *Social Problems* 11 (1964): 66.

55. See J. W. Hurst, *Law and Economic Growth* (Cambridge: Harvard University Press, 1964), p. 345; and F. Pollock and F. W. Maitland, *History of English Law*, vol. 2 (Cambridge: Cambridge University Press, 1968), pp. 577-78. See also J. Hall, *Law, Theft and Society* (Boston: Little, Brown, 1935).

56. See A. R. Lindensmith, *The Addict and the Law* (Bloomington, Ind.: University of Indiana Press, 1967).

57. See Doreen McBarnett, "Law and Capital," *International Journal of the Sociology of Law* 12 (1984): 231-38.

which interacts with itself, its ways of doing things, so that what is possible is limited. The law is a social institution as well as a set of practices characterized by the distinctive features of the legal form, the role of cases, and decision making in concrete and particular situations. This is what E. P. Thompson meant when he described law as a mediating instrument reinforcing and legitimating, masking and mystifying social relations and class rule.[58] Politics may also mediate and mask social relations, but law does so differently. The difference—what we recognize as the legal form and the central focus of the institution—is what is interesting to the practitioner of the sociology of law and what must be considered in any attempt to connect law with other social phenomena—community, justice, or morality.

III

Sociological studies of law have traditionally been pursued outside of the mainstream of legal discourse, participating at a remove while offering an alternative epistemology and jurisprudence. In this, it has been a critical enterprise, its focus decentering, concerned not with what the law *is*—the concern of legal elites—but with what the law *does*—a concern of users and receivers of law.[59] Although this tradition encompasses a vision of a socially constructed reality, it pays less attention to its own role in constructing that reality, and in particular to the role of social scientists in creating legality.

Sociological inquiry began with a broad but simple claim that institutions, including legal institutions, cannot be understood apart from the context of the entire social environment. At the same time as sociologists have insisted on bringing sociology to law, we have done less well attending to the forces that frame our descriptions of legal institutions and their environments. We have not done very well at promoting a sociology of the sociology of law. The rich and extensive literature describing how legal systems work not only describes what is done through law but

---

58. Thompson, *Whigs and Hunters* (New York: Random House, 1975).

59. See David Trubek, "Where the Action Is: Critical Legal Studies and Empiricism," *Stanford Law Review* 36 (1984): 575.

defines what is possible in law. The descriptive research becomes a variable in the construction of legality because the narratives we create provide plausible understandings that simultaneously limit and constrain what is imagined as possible. As sociological studies of law expose the illusions of the natural vision, they simultaneously create their own illusions.

What is the vision of legality that has been constructed through our empirical studies of law? It has been shaped by a number of choices we made.

First we moved from a concern with the relationship between community and law to an investigation of the relationship between law and society. In this move, we abstracted the social relations that constitute both law and morality from the particular situations and environments in which they were created. We produced a discourse of universality in which there are not communities but a *society*, in which there are not laws but *the law*.[60]

Second, we accepted the political formulation of the distinction between law and society without characterizing that relationship as problematic. Social scientists recognized that society was problematic but failed to characterize as problematic the idea of law itself. We looked for connections between law and society as if the two were separate. They are not. In this tradition, law became either a symbol or artifact, a dependent variable created by social forces or an independent variable, "determin[ing] what is possible in politics."[61] Neither of these positions is sufficient in itself; they end up reifying both society and law rather than conceiving of them as mutually constitutive.

Third, having accepted and reified the distinction between law and society, we set about studying the effectiveness of law in this relationship. Scholars explored the consequences and implementation of law and found, much to their surprise, the ineffectiveness of law, a gap between law on the books and the

---

60. This argument is based upon a more extensive analysis by Susan S. Silbey and Austin Sarat in "Critical Traditions in Law and Society Research," *Law and Society Review* (1987): 165; and Austin Sarat and Susan S. Silbey, "The Pull of the Policy Audience," *Law and Policy* (1988): 97.

61. John Brigham, *Civil Liberties and American Democracy* (Washington: Congressional Quarterly Press, 1984).

"law in action."[62] By focusing on the administration of law, researchers were drawn to hard cases—that is, to instances in which law attempts to alter social arrangements and is most likely to fail. The research paints pictures of a legal system struggling to retain what seems like a tenuous grasp on the social order. It portrays legal officials as vainly struggling against great odds to do law's bidding and thereby effaces the overwhelming reality of lawfulness, of law's contribution to the reproduction and maintenance of existing social relations and practices. Too few studies have focused on this more normal pattern of legal life. Sociolegal research has done little to investigate or demonstrate how law works when it does work, and little to show how problematic both the forms and the consequences of effective legal regulation can be.[63]

Often research is based on the premise that law could and should be made more effective. Like the early American legal realists, sociologists of law often become advocates for legal intervention and promoters of effective legal regulation. What starts out looking like critique almost inevitably ends up in apology. The law itself is seldom questioned. We become technicians for the existing social order, and we help rationalize policy by providing both legitimacy and technical planning.[64]

Thus sociologists of law, perceiving themselves to be marginal or ineffective in the world of legal policy,[65] nonetheless work to maintain the existing legal order. Rarely questioning the basis or adequacy of existing legal institutions and arrangements, researchers act as if the solution for legal problems is to be found within law itself, eagerly participating in what Lenore Weitzman

---

62. See Malcolm Feeley, "The Concept of Laws in Social Science," *Law and Society Review* 10 (1976): 497; Richard Abel, "Redirecting Studies of Law," *Law and Society Review* 14 (1980); David Nelken, "The 'Gap' Problem in the Sociology of Law," *Windsor Access to Justice Yearbook* 1 (1981): 35; and Austin Sarat, "Legal Effectiveness and Social Studies of Law," *Legal Studies Forum* 9 (1985): 23.

63. See Silbey and Bittner, "The Availability of Law."

64. See Herbert Gans, "Social Science for Social Policy," in *The Use and Abuse of Social Science*, 2d ed., ed. Irving Louis Horowitz (New Brunswick, N.J.: Transaction Books, 1975).

65. See Lawrence Friedman, "The Law and Society Movement," *Stanford Law Review* 38 (1986).

has called a continuous process of correction and refinement.[66] Sometimes this leads to calls for more law, as for example in Laura Nader's work on consumer protection,[67] and sometimes it leads to calls for less law, as in Eugene Bardach and Robert Kagan's work on the enforcement of health and safety regulations.[68] It should be noted, however, that although Bardach and Kagan call for less law, they do so out of a concern for state legality: they argue that justice and efficiency would be better served if we lowered our expectations about what law can do.

By accepting the values and assumptions of state legality, scholars ignore the role of law in the organization of social power and as a result fail to investigate the law as field for the play of social power.[69] By attending narrowly to the relative effectiveness of regulation, they overlook the ways in which regulation that fails to achieve its stated purpose (e.g., to make the workplace safer) may nevertheless influence relations between workers and managers, consumers and businessmen by providing resources, strategies, and arenas for contests among groups or interests. Indeed, the focus on effectiveness masks, as it neglects, the contribution of particular laws to the construction of social practices and culture.

If the study of the moral authority of law is to be successful, it will have to proceed on a different path and from another place. Instead of studying the effectiveness of law where it is actively in-

---

66. See, for example, Weitzman's *Divorce Revolution* (New York: Free Press, 1985). In her research on the consequences of "no-fault" divorce in California, Weitzman describes herself as surprised that it has done great damage to women and children and that it has contributed in a significant way, as she puts it, to growing gender inequality and the feminization of poverty. She sees the effects as unanticipated and unintended and therefore wants to help correct the error of past policies. She describes herself as engaged in a "continuous process of correction and refinement," helping policymakers achieve their allegedly benign and admirable objectives. For a more elaborate discussion of this perspective, see Austin Sarat and Susan S. Silbey, "The Pull of the Policy Audience," *Law and Policy* (1988): 97.

67. See Nader, *No Access to Law* (New York: Academic Press, 1980).

68. See Bardach and Kagan, *Going by the Book* (Philadelphia: Temple University Press, 1982).

69. See Dennis Wrong, *Power: Its Forms, Bases, and Uses* (New York: Harper & Row, 1979).

tervening in people's lives, we should look to where it is least visible, where legal culture is being transmitted and learned in such ways that it quietly but routinely channels and shapes attitudes and behavior. Moreover, we should begin by noticing that lawyers have got hold of only part of the law—the part where there is trouble or the anticipation of trouble. The domain of law that lies outside the professional's grasp is what the German legal theorist Eugen Ehrlich calls the living law, what we recognize daily in our untroubled transactions as legal relationships, whether or not they constitute the substance of what lawyers spend much of their time doing.[70] Ehrlich places at the core of legal life those behaviors that lie behind the screen of legislation and decision but actually govern society, though only periodically becoming enacted in formal rules. These norms define the taken-for-granted world of legal practices and legitimacy.

Ehrlich underscores the point that a court trial is an exceptional occurrence in comparison to the innumerable contracts and transactions that are consummated in the daily life of the community. In light of the fact that only small morsels of life come before officials charged with the adjudication of disputes, he argues that we must go beyond the "norms of decision" laid down for adjudication to the "norms of organization" that originate in society and determine actual behavior of the average person who becomes enmeshed in innumerable legal relations.

The law, as Ehrlich understands it, is subjugated to social forces but also serves to shape social forces. Law is both a tool and the raw material of legal actors, a resource that needs to be understood in the wider context of the social relations of which it is merely a part. As a rule, "one pays one's debts and renders to one's employer the performance that is due";[71] one pays the shopkeeper for a tube of toothpaste, and the title is thereby transferred. It is not the threat of adjudication or compulsion by the state that routinely induces a person to perform these duties, although that is certainly a part of the situation. More is at stake than the performance of legally enforceable obligations. Legal forms are consti-

---

70. Ehrlich, *Fundamental Principles of the Sociology of Law,* trans. Walter L. Moll (New York: Arno, 1975).
71. Steven Vago, *Law and Society* (Englewood Cliffs, N.J.: Prentice Hall, 1981), pp. 40-41.

tutive of the forms that social relations and practices take. Law is so embedded in those relations and practices that it is virtually invisible to those involved. It is this invisibility, this taken-for-grantedness, that makes legality and legal forms so powerful.

From this perspective, the dominant views of law as an instrument of state power, the outcome of political and legal struggles, or a complex and historically evolving set of rules and expectations are one-sided and insufficient. In each, the law is impoverished, considered merely an ineffective instrument or a professional technique; the conventional practices and constitutive aspects of law are disregarded. In order to paint a richer, more complex picture, some scholars have begun to view law as a set of cultural and symbolic languages.[72] As a cultural system, "law offers a set of symbols and meanings, stories, rituals, and world-views that people use in varying configurations."[73] It provides a tool kit of habits, skills, and tactics from which people construct strategies of action as well as belief.

IV

In conclusion, let me reiterate my perspective on legal research and attempt to specify the crisis in law. By critiquing the sociological project, I am not suggesting that I wish to reject empiricism or return to a world of idealism. In affirming the social construction of social relations, however, I wish to emphasize the consequences of those constructions and the relations that limit what is possible. I wish to emphasize that the sociology of law is one of those social constructions—as is the natural-law perspective—that limits and contrains what is understood about and possible in law.

Often we sociologists of law write as if we were describing

---

72. See John Brigham, *Constitutional Language* (Westport, Conn.: Greenwood Press, 1978); Timothy O'Neill, "The Language of Equality in a Constitutional Order," *American Political Science Review* 75 (1981): 626; Timothy O'Neill, *Law as Metaphor* (forthcoming); Carol Greenhouse, "Nature Is to Culture as Praying Is to Suing," *Journal of Legal Pluralism* 20 (1982): 20; and "Interpreting American Litigiousness," paper presented at the Law and Society Association annual meeting, San Diego, June 1985.

73. Ann Swidler, "Culture in Action: Symbols and Strategies," *American Sociological Review* 51 (1986): 273.

an objective but nonetheless manipulable world of social relations; indeed, this is what we mean by "social reality."[74] But the task and the interest of scholarship are to observe (and perhaps critique) the processes of constructing that world, including the construction of legality. The goal of social research is not, I think, to take the perspective of the actor as the standard of inquiry but to make that perspective and epistemology the subject of inquiry. This distinction emphasizes the difference between technocratic and critical research. It requires that we observe our own participation in that process. It demands that we explore the politics that have been embedded in the traditions of legal studies—the focus on the state, the benign view of lawmakers, and the refusal to evaluate legal goals.

One of the claims I have made is that studies of law should move from both the natural-law vision and the instrumental sociological vision of law to something more akin to Erhlich's notion of the living law, to the ways in which law constitutes social life rather than works to alter or change it. It is very possible that in this perspective I have overestimated the effectiveness and stability of legal forms, just as social scientists have heretofore overstated the ineffectiveness of law. It would be more appropriate, then, not to look solely at either the efforts of legal instrumentality and change or at the hegemonic realm of conformity but rather at the ways in which issues, people, and problems move from one domain to the other. With renewed attention to the role of intellectual resources, the stock of established expertise, and the symbols available to citizens as well as to agents of the state, we can observe the struggles to move from one arena to the other. My word of caution, however, is that we must also take care to note the role that we as scholars and scientists play in this movement, in the social construction of law and legality.

---

74. People commonly assume the existence of an intersubjectively known yet external and accessible world in their "natural attitude" as competent members of society. See Alfred Schutz, *On Phenomenology and Social Relations* (Chicago: University of Chicago Press, 1970); and Berger and Luckmann, *The Social Construction of Reality*. Melvin Pollner has said that the notion of "one single world" knowable by any competent person is the "incorrigible assumption" of social life ("The Very Coinage of Your Brain: The Anatomy of Reality Disjunctures," *Philosophy of the Social Sciences* 5 [1975]: 411).

The Tension between Law in America and the Religious Tradition

Thomas L. Shaffer

> *We need a communal instrument of moral reasoning in the light of faith precisely to defend the decision-maker against the stream of conformity to his own world's self-evidence. Practical moral reasoning, if Christian, must always be expected to be at some point subversive.*
>
> —John Howard Yoder

The only useful way I know even to begin to consider tensions between the religious tradition and the law is to describe the religious tradition from within, as it has understood itself.

The religious tradition in our culture has not understood itself as a philosophy or a preference or a point of view. It has understood itself as a sequence of facts that those in the tradition learn to remember. Faithfulness to the tradition depends on truthful memory rather than intellectual justification. The religious tradition is not a subculture, not a "world within the world," not a constituency. Its principal mandate is to preserve in memory — in teaching, ritual, calendar, and narrative — a sequence of events, a "master story."

The religious tradition is what is remembered by a particular people. I want to suggest in this paper—suggest for discussion— that the tensions I have been asked to describe occur for two reasons: (1) because this particular remembering people is wary of circumstances that might impair its memory, and (2) because this particular remembering people knows something about the destiny of human persons.[1]

The religious end of the tension is a story and a picture. The story and the picture (in one characteristic event) show the children of Israel assembled on the borders of Canaan. Moses says to them, "You are a people consecrated to the Lord your God; of all the peoples on earth the Lord your God chose you to be the treasured people" (Deut. 7:6, Jewish Publication Society translation).

This is a powerless people, decimated by plague and battle, by discord, and by a generation of wandering and living hand to mouth in the desert. One of its two principal leaders, Aaron, is dead. The other, Moses, is dying. But Moses tells the children of Israel that they are to *consume* the more numerous people that already live in Canaan. Israel is then to take over the land and to hold it as a treasure and a promise from God himself.

They are not to *adapt:* "You shall not intermarry with them. . . . You shall tear down their altars, smash their pillars, cut down their sacred posts, and consign their images to the fire. . . . You shall not worship their gods. . . . You shall consign the images of their gods to the fire; you shall not covet the silver and gold on them and keep it for yourselves . . . for that is abhorrent to the Lord your God" (Deut. 7:5, 16, 25, J.P.S. translation). Is-

---

1. I understand or define our "religious tradition" to mean the Hebraic tradition, the tradition of Jews and Christians. The position I take in this introduction is developed in Julian N. Hartt's *Christian Critique of American Culture* (New York: Harper & Row, 1967), and in Michael Goldberg's *Jews and Christians: Getting Our Stories Straight* (Nashville: Abingdon, 1985). Says Hartt, "The church does not behave faithfully when it tries to make the Resurrection somehow intellectually digestible, if not exactly palatable, for the refined sensitivities of contemporary man (who has buried enough victims of his modernity to have little stomach for meeting them all face to face sometime). Rather, the faithful church interprets what man is and ought to become in the light of the Resurrection. If someday we all must be confronted by every last one of our victims, many of whom we could not name if we wanted to, it is only because God who brought Jesus Christ from the dead loves them and loves all with the infinite love which will prevail even over our mortal guilt."

rael is to be—as it was, and as it is—a particular people in Canaan and among the nations.

The Gentiles who later became the Christian church laid claim to this particularity. Their story and their picture is the Cross, which is a symbol both of what the nations do to Jews and of what people do to one another in the name of the law.

Jesus before the power of Rome and Moses at the borders of Canaan are signs of insistence on particularity rather than on power: power is inexplicable. Power is God's business. Moses tells Israel at the borders of Canaan to remember—and, remembering, to obey. He tells them that the purpose of their testing in the desert is neither athletic nor moral but is to prepare them to live in dependence on God.[2] He tells them that the occupants of Canaan will be dislodged only little by little. As it turns out, the Canaanites were not destroyed so much as they were assimilated—which is what happened to the Romans, too. The Torah does not say the Canaanites were to be destroyed; it says they were to be consumed.[3]

So this particular people—the religious end of the tension between religion and law—has mostly to *be* what it is, a particular people "at odds with dominant assumptions . . . chosen, summoned, commanded . . . promised . . . concrete and specific . . . who know so well who they are that they value and celebrate their oddity in the fact of every seductive and powerful imperial imperative."[4]

What is the legal end of the tension between law and the religious tradition? Let me make the tentative suggestion that the law, in a modern American lawyer's sense, may be in Canaan. The particular people would then be wary of the law. They have been told to be wary of it, because the law in Canaan may be a

---

2. There have been centuries of rabbinical sermons on the difference between the *goy kadosh* (holy nation) of Exodus 19:6 and the *am kadosh* of Deuteronomy 28:9. Israel in the desert, in its struggle with God, had begun as a holy *nation,* but it emerged at the borders of Canaan as a holy *people.*

3. The command to consume the Canaanites is, of course, a matter of extensive ethical speculation—then and now; see Luke Lea, "The Torah and the West Bank," *Judaism* 36 (1987): 264.

4. Walter Brueggemann, "Passion and Perspective: Two Dimensions of Education in the Bible," *Theology Today* 42 (1985): 172.

god: You shall not worship their gods! You shall not even be curious about their gods (Deut. 12:30). The radical questions for the particular people are whether the law, in American liberal democracy, is in Canaan; and, if there, is it an idol?

Idols in this imagery are things the Canaanites make with their hands—including, perhaps, wooden figures that can be carried around, as Queequeg carried his little god into his room at the inn on Nantucket, where he prayed to it and Ishmael watched in horror. Ishmael was on the borders of Canaan in that room at the inn; he tried at first not to be curious about this little wooden god. The shifting images—from Canaan to Nantucket and back again—suggest a point: the things of Canaan need not be abhorrent unless they are idols; the idols of Canaan are abhorrent only so long as they *are* idols; and what makes them idols is how the Canaanites feel about them.

There came a time, after Israel was established in Canaan, when Israelites came up with Canaanite artifacts and wanted to keep them as antiques and mementos (as our parents kept Nazi military decorations). Some of these Canaanite artifacts had been idols (perhaps they were like Queequeg's little wooden god). The rabbis had to decide whether the discoverers of these artifacts could possess them, in view of the stern injunction Moses gave Israel at the borders of Canaan. The ruling was that the artifact could be kept by the Israelite who had it even if it had been an idol, if it could be shown that it had been repudiated by the person for whom it had been an idol. Was the artifact, for example, mutilated? The artifact could be kept only if the Canaanite who had once worshiped it had himself turned from worshiping it, had repudiated it. Mutilation would be favorable evidence of repudiation.

If that distinction can be appropriated on this question of tension between the legal tradition and the religious tradition, the outcome will be this: the particular people is wary of the law in Canaan; it may be an idol, but it is not necessarily so, and if it is not, the particular people need not be so wary. The way you find out whether the law is an idol is to see if the people for whom it is the law have come to worship it. If they haven't, then the law has no particular danger for the particular people.[5]

---

5. Sometimes when reading the conservative side of the argument over the critical legal studies movement, I see signs of idolatry—or, at

The wariness I am talking about is not entirely mythic. It is evident in the pastoral letter on the American economy completed by the Roman Catholic Bishops of the United States in November 1986. American liberal democracy is for the bishops a medium, as is our modified capitalistic economy. The bishops seem to have found that our democracy and economy are not idols (although perhaps they have been), but they are—and here the bishops are relentlessly ambivalent—alien. The letter speaks, for example, of believers *going out into* the economy. They speak of the "virtues of citizenship" as compatible with faith, but they also insist on the traditional distinction in Catholic thought between society and the state. Finally they hold out a vision for humankind that is neither American nor republican but messianic.[6] "The church," they say, "is not bound to any particular economic, political or social system; it has lived with many . . . evaluating each according to moral and ethical principles" based on the Hebraic understanding that human dignity is a higher value than either prosperity or individual rights, that community is a higher value than individual autonomy, and that the moral minimum for the person in a just society is not economic freedom but adequate material and personal participation in common life. The bishops neither endorse nor offer a system; they identify the system we have as pragmatic, and they judge it in terms of whether it allows the particular people to search here for justice. They mean by justice what the Hebrew prophets meant, not what Mr. Jefferson meant.

My agenda now is to suggest some ways to analyze the tension. Four ways seem evident to me as I look at Israel and Canaan, at the Roman gibbet and the Jewish followers of Jesus who stand looking at the gibbet:

    1. There is the business of Canaan tending to Canaan, of

---

least, I cannot find evidence of mutilation. See my comment in "Levinson Builds the Kingdom: Comment on Professing Law," *St. Louis University Law Journal* 31 (1986): 73.

    6. "The Christian vision is based on the conviction that God has destined the human race and all creation for 'a kingdom of truth and life, of holiness and grace, of justice, love and peace'" (from the preface of the Mass for the Feast of Christ the King).

    Caesar tending to Caesar, of what the government is to do about the government.

2. There is the business of the particular people tending to itself, of what, in Christian terms, the church is to do about the church.

3. There is the government doing something about the church.

4. There is the church doing something about the government.

I. WHAT IS THE GOVERNMENT TO DO ABOUT THE GOVERNMENT?

The first of these is the enterprise of American lawyers: What is the government to do about the government? Government and the economy it regulates are the apparatus, the *institution,* within American liberal democracy, and the tending (or mocking or subverting) of that institution is the business of lawyers. We lawyers are, as Tocqueville noticed a century and a half ago, the only American aristocracy. Fussing about the government is, always and everywhere, the business of the American legal aristocracy. I don't propose to discuss this first agenda; I want only to notice that discussing it has become the usual daily business of law teachers.

II. WHAT IS THE CHURCH TO DO ABOUT THE CHURCH?

The second way to analyze the tension is one I do need to pause over. The issue is what the church is to do about the church. It becomes an issue for this essay because of the nature of the claim the particular people makes. What is Israel's claim at the borders of Canaan? What is the nature of the claim the Christian church made when it appropriated for the Gentiles the particularity of Israel? What is most important for me to say about this is that the claim of particularity is not a claim to power or to a right to power. It has nothing to do with *rights;* it is a matter of faithfulness to memory.[7] Israel *hears,* in the classic prayer of the Torah.

---

7. Why, then, is it even a "claim"? To take this memory up as a claim is to acknowledge in some way that the religious tradition feels it

Israel hears what God has done and what he has insisted upon; it hears in order to remember slavery in Egypt, and Exodus, and Sinai. Its particularity is that it hears and remembers. Theology in the church is also memory in this way: theology is, as Bonhoeffer said, the memory of the church. Particularity is memory and faithfulness but not a moral boast, not a claim to have *fulfilled* the expectations of God. Not the memory that those expectations have been fulfilled—we know they have not been—and not a claim that the particular people fulfills them now. Jews pray, on the Day of Atonement, "[We] are not so arrogant and stiffnecked as to say . . . [that] we . . . have not sinned." The particularity of the people of God is normative, but it is not the boast that the particular people is obedient, nor the claim that it has been obedient.

That point about boasting is important, because the claim of particularity has to take history into account. Israel and the church have failed; their particular history and their particular histories are histories of failure, of disobedience, and of abandonment. Moses said to Israel at the borders of Canaan, "From the day that you left the land of Egypt until you reached this place, you have continued defiant toward the Lord." The particular people is stiff-necked, as Jewish Scripture and Christian Scripture say; but still it learns to remember that it is a particular people. When the children of Israel worshiped the golden calf, God said he would destroy them and give to Moses a new people. But Moses argued for the only people he had: What would a *new* people be like? His argument was even that this people was the only people *God* had: What would a new people be like for God? What would the nations say about what God did to the old people? Moses' argument, which was successful, was that not

---

necessary to justify itself before "the nations." I think that is true today; it may not have been true for either Moses or the primitive church. But it is true, at least in well-settled habit, of the religious tradition in America. The reason I use the language of *claim* here is not to accede to a demand for Kantian justification; it is only to attempt to expand on what I mean by particularity. My purpose is therefore part of the issue of the church tending to the church, of Israel being Israel. What I want mostly to suggest is that this is not the government's business, that when the church has made this particularly the government's business, it has not been faithful.

even God could disown this particular people (Exod. 32; Deut. 9–10).

This tangent on what the church should do about the church is affirmatively important to my thesis about tension between the religious tradition and law for two reasons. The first reason has to do with one kind of failure in the religious tradition—one among many kinds: the people of God have failed to remember who they are and have surrendered their particularity to the government. Israel did this when it demanded a king, the early church when it baptized Constantine, the medieval church with its pagan theories of church and state, the congregational church in the Reformation when it turned its procedures over to local government and, in the name of order, abandoned the procedures it had discovered in the New Testament. Particular people and the particular people itself failed its memory in many ways; the way that is most relevant to what I want to say about the tension between law and religion is that the particular people decided that it was responsible for the government and the government was responsible for it.

The other point I want to make about the importance of what the church is to do about the church is that particularity includes attention to the processes by which people within the church deal with one another. This, again, is not a matter of moral or communal superiority; it is not a matter of civil liberties, nor of a philosophical view of the human person. It is a matter of remembering how God told the particular people to conduct its own business: with curiosity about one another, with openness. The reason for this openness, I think, is that the God of Israel comes to people in the community, in other people. In Israel, and in the teaching of Jesus and of St. Paul, teaching authority depends upon the observance of an "open congregational process" (so says Yoder; cf. the allusions to authority in the bishops' letter). The particular people is not dependent on an establishment—that is, on any sort of institution guaranteed by coerced order—but on listening to one another, on what Yoder calls the "communal quality of belief." When the procedure is observed—as it is observed, for example, in post-Talmudic Judaism—validity is sought not in a liberal-democratic "marketplace of ideas" but in the presence of God (Matt. 18).

The Midrash illustrates what an "open congregational

process" is among the Jews. On an issue involving levitical purity, Rabbi Eliezer argued and argued but didn't convince the others in his House of Study. He called on a carob tree to prove him right, and the carob tree moved, miraculously. He called on a stream of water, and it began to flow backwards. Eliezer's colleagues said that a carob tree and a stream of water cannot serve as proof. Eliezer called on the walls of the House of Study, and the walls began to lean downward. Rabbi Joshua said to the walls, "What business is it of yours?" and the walls stopped moving. (However, out of respect for Rabbi Eliezer, the walls did not move back to where they had been.) Rabbi Eliezer then called on God himself, and a voice came from heaven saying that Rabbi Eliezer was right. Rabbi Joshua got to his feet and said, quoting the Torah (Deut. 30:12), "It is not in the heavens!"[8] Later, Rabbi Jeremiah said this meant that the Torah had been given on Mount Sinai, once and for all, and after that it was for God's people to decide what the words of Torah meant. Rabbi Nathan was told by the prophet Elijah that God heard the argument Rabbi Joshua made that day, and God said, "My children have prevailed against me!"

That midrash establishes the relevant jurisdiction, but it does not explicate procedure. For this, there is another midrash, one that involves an argument between the School of Shammai and the School of Hillel and that occurred a short time before the birth of Jesus. In this case, the voice from heaven said that both schools were proclaiming the words of God but that the law should be decided according to the School of Hillel. And the scholars wondered how that could be: If both schools taught the words of God, why should one prevail over the other? The Talmud says it was because the sages of Hillel were tolerant, friendly, and modest. "They studied not only their own traditions, but also those of the School of Shammai. Indeed, they transmitted the teachings of the School of Shammai before they transmitted their own teachings."

---

8. In context: "For this Law that I enjoin on you today is not beyond your strength or beyond your reach. It is not in heaven, so that you need to wonder, 'Who will cross the seas for us and bring it back to us, so that we may hear it and keep it?' No, the Word is very near to you, it is in your mouth and in your heart for your observance" (Deut. 30:11-14, Jerusalem Bible).

III. WHAT IS THE GOVERNMENT TO DO ABOUT THE CHURCH?

I am talking about tensions between law and the religious tradition. The third way I have suggested for doing that is to ask what the government is to do about the church. What the government usually wants to do about the church is to appropriate its energy—to turn religion into civil religion, to turn democracy into a religion—and otherwise to keep the church either under control or irrelevant. This third issue is narrowly comprehended by the branch of legal study called church-and-state law, or the law of religion. The main thing I want to argue about church and state is that it is the government's problem, not the church's. Moses did not tell the spies who had checked out Canaan for him to ask the Canaanites what they thought about Israel's mandate from God. He did not negotiate on the matter of the idols—and he would have if he had really been interested in being responsible for a peaceful and religious public order. Some accommodation on the matter of idols would evidently have saved the successors of Moses from war, civil strife, and apostasy: it would have served the evident interests of both law and religion. But Moses did not negotiate. His mandate was to consume the people and destroy their idols.

There was a sort of security investigation of potential converts in the primitive (Roman) church, in which the person seeking baptism was asked if he had anything to do with the government—whether, for example, he was a soldier or a judge. If he was, he was told he would have to give up being a soldier or a judge. If he wanted to keep his imperial office, he was denied baptism. It would have made sense—as it did later, after Constantine—to have baptized a general or two, and lots of judges. It would have led to a more religious and more peaceful public order. But the fathers of the church saw the issue as Moses saw the idols of Canaan: the business of the church is to remember and to celebrate its oddity.[9] The Jews, then and now, will show us Christians how that is done.

---

9. They did, and those who survived were successful, for a while, at being odd. See Robert L. Wilken, *The Christians as the Romans Saw Them* (New Haven: Yale University Press, 1984).

An analogy can be found in the situation of groups of workers in Britain and America. Such groups began, two hundred years ago, in community, and no doubt they began with the memory of their particularity as religious people. The communities in which they began were civil and economic (i.e., all of the workers in a place), and they were also "professional" (i.e., related to a particular kind of work—a "practice," perhaps, in the way Aristotelians use that word). They sought, as "industrial democracy" formed itself within liberal democracy, to exercise collective influence—and, almost as soon as they began to do that, they were condemned by the government on the ground that they were coercive. They were understood—correctly, I think—as making a radical challenge to the anthropology of liberal democracy, the anthropology that says each of us is radically alone and each of us is best served through governmental guarantees of individual autonomy. The community of workers is understood—correctly, I think—as subversive of republican government and heretical within the orthodoxy of Enlightenment politics.

The legal rhetoric with which these challenges from associations of workers were met was the rhetoric of coercion: it is illegitimate to interpose a collective moral authority between the republic and any of its citizens. The legal rubric for this included charges that associations of workers were common-law criminal conspiracies and that they interfered with common-law freedom of contract. But the meaning of the legal charges was that these associations were an illegitimate locus of power within liberal democracy.

The resolution of the difficulty in modern industrial democracies was that these associations of workers were appropriated by the government. They function now through state-supervised elections. The organic character they once had, through the commonality of being in a community or through the commonality of sharing a skill or even through common political purposes, has been sacrificed to the state's interest in the orderly production of commodities and in industrial peace. Under the label of its interest in civil liberties, the state now supervises even the relation between a labor association and each of its members, one curious feature of which is a legal distinction between the interests of the members of the association and the association's "ideological activities" (*Abood v. Detroit Board of Education,* 431 U.S. 209, 236, 1977): wages are the business of state-supervised labor unions; ideology is not.

The swap that labor made is one that appears to have resolved an often violent tension between workers and the government, but one can also read modern labor history as a history of government intrusion into the lives of organic communities. "Government impinged on working-class life in the family, the neighborhood, and the factory, and in schools, parks, and saloons."[10] Government did all of this by securing itself from the "ideological activities" that had formed the associations in the first place—"from their subversive moral reasoning," in Yoder's phrase.

The analogy I labor to suggest here is that the religious tradition has a similar tendency to trade its particularity for security and influence. In labor's case, one can detect an argument now beginning to be made by labor-law scholars, that the situation of workers in America is more alienated from American business enterprise than it was at the beginning of our industrial history. The worker in America is, in the reigning theories of what a business enterprise is, more a commodity than he was when my great-grandfather came from Ireland to Kentucky to work in the coal mines.

The Roman Catholic bishops address a similar issue when they speak to business managers in terms of trusteeship and vocation. The beneficiaries of these trusts the bishops mention are not all or even principally the investment bankers who manipulate capital on Wall Street. The vocation is not, when seen truthfully, a call only to earn profit for investors. But if you look even casually at labor law, or securities law, or the developing law that regulates manipulations of investor power, you find it hard to detect any principled difference between a worker and a robot. I want to suggest that there is a useful analogy between associations of workers surrendering themselves to the government and

---

10. Craig Becker, review of Tomlins's "The State and the Unions," *Harvard Law Review* 100 (1987): 672. The Roman Catholic bishops seem to me to have missed this fact; they persist in regarding modern American labor organizations not as institutions, and in fact institutions largely under the control of the government, so much as organic associations of workers.

the perennial tendency of religious associations to trade their particularity for security and influence. In each case the radical claim is a claim about memory, and in each case—as the bishops put it—moral substance has to do with the dignity of persons in communities more than with rights in a system of public order.

IV. WHAT IS THE CHURCH TO DO ABOUT THE GOVERNMENT?

The fourth issue I want to talk about, in response to the invitation to talk about the tension between law and the religious tradition, is What is the church to do about the government?

There are two responses to that question in the religious tradition. The first is that the particular people will not bow down to the government's idols. This is a significant limitation for participation in American liberal democracy, a limitation that has often been violated by believers.[11] Thomas Jefferson referred to America as God's new Israel; that is not what America is. (Abraham Lincoln shook his head over such rhetoric and said we Americans were God's almost-chosen people.) Jefferson's phrase and phrases like it ("a city on a hill," "the righteous empire") have been an invitation to idolatry that some Jews and Christians have accepted and some have not.

David Hoffman, the founder of American legal ethics and an eloquent Jeffersonian as well as a Christian, spoke of American law as a temple and of lawyers as priests who served in the temple. "Ministers at a holy altar," he called us. Some of the later excesses of the social gospel movement, particularly the claim

---

11. Political theology is, of course, a discursive subject within the family of believers. Pastor Neuhaus and my friend and mentor Stanley Hauerwas argue about it (see Neuhaus, *The Naked Public Square: Religion and Democracy in America* [Grand Rapids: Eerdmans, 1984], and Hauerwas, *Against the Nations: War and Survival in a Liberal Society* [San Francisco: Harper & Row, 1985]). Their argument is within and, as far as I can tell, controlled by the internal processes I describe above (see Yoder, *The Priestly Kingdom: Social Ethics as Gospel* [Notre Dame, Ind.: University of Notre Dame Press, 1984]). I have attempted to assay the jurisprudence of this intrafamilial discussion in "Jurisprudence in the Light of Hebraic Faith," *Notre Dame Journal of Law, Ethics, and Public Policy* 1 (1984): 77.

that American democracy *was* the church, were even worse.[12] Those were failures within the particular people that the church claims to be. At such times, and as a consequence of such times, the faithful have had sometimes to say, with Thoreau, that the best people are in jail. It is not a quaint issue, nor an altogether historical issue: it has been the moral (and even political) substance of the long, careful pastoral letters that have issued from church leadership (in most of the "mainline" Christian denominations) in the last five years—letters, particularly, about the worship of nuclear weapons and worship of the capitalist economy. Worship—bowing down to idols—is the issue discussed in those pastoral documents.

The other response to the question of what the church is to do about the government is the response the religious tradition calls prophetic—appropriating for itself the style and purpose of the Hebrew prophets. This response appropriates the religious tradition's most ancient understanding of why it *is* a particular people: Israel and the church are a particular people in order to bring the one God to all of mankind. This people is among the nations for purposes of leadership and atonement. The chosen people is a hard-hearted and stiff-necked people and, in that, reflects the sinfulness and stubbornness of humankind. Israel is sinful and stubborn on the borders of Canaan; the church has been sinful and stubborn in, say, its recurrent spasms of hatred of the Jews and its craven failure during the Holocaust.[13]

But the particular people is more than representative of humankind; it is also the agent of atonement: it returns—it is able to return—and in turning *(teshuvah)* to witness, to covenant and mitzvot, it atones for all of humankind. It is prophet and priest; it atones for itself and, vicariously, for the world. The notion of vicarious atonement has been prominent and troublesome in the church, but it is a notion the church appropriated from the Torah. Moses did it first; Moses went up and down the slopes of

---

12. I have been helped on this point by Jan C. Dawson's essay "The Religion of Democracy in Early Twentieth-Century America," *Journal of Church and State* 27 (1985): 46.

13. Finally, I suppose, this stiff-necked stubbornness and moral failure is a *comfort* to the world. As one of President Carter's friends said, explaining Southern Baptist theology, "People are a bunch of bastards, but God loves them anyway."

Sinai after God said he would destroy all of Israel and give Moses a *new* people. Moses fasted for 120 days and prostrated himself in the dust and argued and changed the mind of God. Israel was not destroyed. Moses was successful. He atoned; he brought Israel and the Lord back to at-one-ment.

A generation later, when Moses told the people who were about to enter Canaan about what he had done at Sinai, he spoke to them as if they had all been there, as if *they* had worshiped the golden calf. But they had not been there! The people Moses spoke to on the borders of Canaan were the children and grandchildren of those who had worshiped the calf. Moses was an old, old man; he was about to die. The people who heard him there were different people, but they were the same particular people. They have listened to the agent of their atonement and they have understood—some of them, some of their Jewish children, and some of their Christian children—that his being prophet and priest for them was a model of their being prophet and priest for all of mankind, suffering servants, as Isaiah put it, servants of the Lord.

So the position of the particular people—the "religious tradition"—in American liberal democracy is a tradition first of wariness and refusal and then of prophecy and atonement. Caution and witness. Those are the notions—the stories, I think— that indicate for the church what the church is to do about the government.

A. Caution

If one wants examples of caution in the religious tradition's approach to the law, I suppose such issues as abortion, capital punishment, nuclear weapons, and the obsession (a sort of negative idolatry) of the current federal government with East-West international polity at the expense of North-South polity, and therefore at the expense of human dignity, are all examples. Stanley Hauerwas speaks thus of the people and institutions in America which claim "that Christians . . . must be willing to choose sides and kill in order to preserve the social orders in which they find themselves."

He goes on to say that "as Christians, when we accept that alternative it surely means that we are no longer the church that witnesses to God's sovereignty over all nations, but instead we have become part of the world," part of Canaan, kneeling to Canaan's idols. Hauerwas's position is the one I identify as caution in the particular people. When the religious tradition, or some significant part of it, takes a position that refuses, as Hauerwas puts it, "to step aside with the world," the tenor of the religious position taken is caution, wariness, distrust lest what the world offers is an idol.

B. Witness

The other way of describing the tension between the religious tradition and American law, the way of witness, is more promising for discourse. I would like to explore the promise of that other way in reference to an example: the situation of the communities in America that aggregate wealth, build empires, and employ people for the production of goods and services—the business corporations.

I have scratched my head for some time—both out of narrow professional interest and in talking as a scholar with scholars—over the situation of the people who preside over these communities, the situation of the managers and directors of corporate businesses, and this particularly in reference to the manipulations of investor power that are involved in struggles for corporate control. I want to suggest for discussion that such people are a focus for the tensions between the religious tradition and American law, and this particularly in reference to the way the religious tradition reaches out from itself not with caution but with prophetic witness.

Most of the energy of a modern American law teacher is given to training young people who plan to serve such enterprises, as lawyers. But very little of our energy, so given, is directed to them as people working in communities where prophetic witness might be possible, let alone to the substance of the prophetic witness. I suppose the main reason that part of the agenda is neglected is a matter of safety. In a modern law school, prophetic witness is not an easy thing to explicate.[14] Our part of

---

14. I speak of *schools*. Law firms are not nearly so blind, as I try to show in a chapter called "The Profession" in my book *Faith and the Professions* (Albany: State University of New York Press, 1987).

the academy more than any other, even the commerce school, has systematically—theologically!—discounted, discouraged, and disapproved of the invocation of the religious tradition as important or even as interesting.

So I must ask the reader who teaches law to suspend disbelief and think about a business manager as a person who might be influenced—even through her lawyers—by the particular people's faithfulness, by its remembering that this people does not bow down to the idols of Canaan, but more especially in its remembering that it is a light to the nations, the salt of the earth. If we can agree that such an influence is alive in this business manager, then we can see her as remembering a story that might show us what the tensions between law and the religious tradition are like. Not an example or an illustration—because that would be to use this person I'm thinking about as if she were a calculator for interest balancing, for costs and benefits. I want to think about her instead as a person who stumbles and strives, who fails and has triumphs, including failures and triumphs she doesn't even see for what they are. An integrated moral person, in other words—on, as Auden said, a moral planet, tamed by terror.

This person is spoken to by the religious tradition in one or both of two ways. She is, first of all, addressed as one of the particular people. She may not think of herself in that way. We may not think of her in that way: I don't recall from the 1950s that the young Jews who were murdered and buried in a dam in Mississippi were talked about as having done what they did because they were Jews. But I think they did. It is no accident but is rather evidence of the presence of God that while American Jews are not the most prominent or the wealthiest group in America, they are, consistently, the most generous in support of charity with their money, their time, and their courage.

We didn't talk, in the 1960s, about the immolations of Dag Hammarskjöld and Martin Luther King, Jr., as immolations of Christians; but that is what they were—as, perhaps, we now know better than we did then. The altruism of believers *can* be taken to be the ordinary exercise of civic goodwill, and often the contributors prefer to have their altruism taken that way. (Dr. King was, I think, an exception.) But, pursued more deeply, they are the actions of members of the particular people; they are the ordinary, daily way that members of a particular people figure out how to live in Canaan and still live within the memory of the particular people. We know that for sure only when we probe the stories of the contributors, as we did in Hammarskjöld's "Markings," but it is always a possibility—and it may be more common—in lives lived far from the madding crowd.

This is not to argue that every decent action we see is, when probed deeply, a mitzvah; but it is to argue that many of them are, and to suggest that ordinary goodness may be a sign of the tension between the religious tradition and the law—sometimes with devotion and with a prayer, no doubt, but more often because almost all of us are affected by the particularity of the Jews and the church. Affected even for the better.

This business person has a vulnerability to religious tradition because of where she comes from, and where she comes from speaks to her about how she should go about being the manager of a corporate business enterprise. The recent letter from the Roman Catholic bishops may cause her, for example, to remember that her position is a *vocation*. She is *called* to do what she is doing, and what she is doing is administering wealth that has been assembled by and from the labor of others. Called by whom? We Catholics used to use the word *vocation* to mean those called to the sisterhood or the priesthood; it meant a personal, oral message from God. I think it usually came in a dream. The bishops seem to give the word a different (even "sectarian") emphasis. I think they are talking about being called out of the church, sent out from the particular people, to do something that is religiously important.

The bishops did not shrink from spelling out (remembering) the implications of being called out of the church to manage a business: the maximization of profit is not the primary goal of the business, they said; profit is not preferred to the dignity and well-being of the persons and communities involved in the business (this with reference to technological innovation or moving to the Sun Belt or with reference to the corporate community's response to an external bid for corporate control).

To remember that business management is a vocation and a trust is to notice the tension between law and the religious tradition. "In the U.S. *law*," the bishops said, "the primary responsibility of managers is to exercise prudent business judgment in the interest of a profitable return to investors. But *morally* this legal responsibility may be exercised only within the bounds of justice to employees, customers, suppliers and the local community. Corporate mergers and hostile takeovers may bring greater benefits to shareholders, but they often lead to decreased concern for the well-being of local communities and make towns and cities more vulnerable to decisions made from afar."

This is not a liberal-democratic argument. It is not primarily an argument made to "human experience and reason." It is not primarily *any* kind of argument, so much as it is a memory relevant to corporate law, within the particular people the bishops claim to be teachers in. Teachers within this people are agents of memory. But this episcopal position on corporate business as a vocation and a trust is also a broad proposition. It has to do with community; the bishops point out that the corporate business enterprise *is* a community. The influence the religious tradition exercises on this management person is a communal influence. It is the influence of neighborhood and family as well as religious congregation.[15] Because of those aspects of her formation she knows what a community is and she knows how to want to be in a community with those in her business enterprise. Her ordinary bent—which the bishops claim for their religious memory—is to regard her business as an organic community and to act for the welfare of that community.

She can be corrupted, of course, so that she comes to act mostly for the preservation of her own power; but when she is not corrupted she acts from the motivation that the religious tradition calls "the common good." You can talk about the common good only from some substantive memory of what "common" means; and what the bishops are after is such a memory in America—not from the Enlightenment or from Mr. Jefferson's vision of a nation of people who would be good because they would be prosperous but from the religious tradition.

The religious tradition has an exact quarrel here with American law, and the bishops assert it clearly: The law directs the corporate manager to an immoral course of action. She is called to be a trustee for those whose labor has produced the

---

15. That was the thrust of Bellah's *Habits of the Heart,* but I think the authors there understated the differences between the religious tradition and civil religion.

wealth she manages. Some of these are employees, some customers; some live in the communities where the business operates, and some have invested their money in the business. A trustee is faithful to all of her beneficiaries. To prefer one and neglect the others is to betray her trust.

The bishops also turn this point into a moral argument, using the same words from the religious tradition—the words *vocation* and *trust*. It is, as an argument, made from reason and experience. Perhaps it is even an argument that could be made from within the legal tradition (although American law just now is less likely to talk about faithfulness than about balancing interests in a system of social costs and benefits). The way the bishops speak of trust is, for example, reminiscent of the way the chancellors spoke of the duty of a trustee in the law of trusts: the trustee has to be faithful to the competing demands of his beneficiaries. The beneficiary who is to receive principal after a life or a period of time will, for example, demand trust investments that preserve and increase principal; the beneficiary who receives current income demands investments that bring high income. The trustee's legal duty is to be faithful to both beneficiaries.

I think this argument, when made from the law (or from reason and experience), lacks a depth that the religious tradition is able to remember—the depth that realizes that a trustee's duty is tragic. The religious tradition is able to bear the possibility that the call to be a trustee (in, say, a corporate business) is a call to tragedy. I don't mean here so much grand Greek tragedies (although those may come) as I mean the ordinary, daily, bitter tragedies of laying people off from their jobs, of asking workers to take less pay, of deciding against a dividend that investors need. Faithfulness to trust involves ordinary tragedies like those, and Israel and the people of the Cross know they do; their memory includes tragedy much more prominently than it includes triumph.

What the particular people remember about tragedy is that, finally, fate is benign. Fate is the father who loves his children. Speaking out of the memory that is the religious tradition, not out of the Greek dramatic and philosophical tradition, Stanley Hauerwas says that tragedy is the triumph of meaning over power, of vocation and trust within a community that seeks the dignity of persons. One could say that reason and experience and law can call a trustee to faithfulness, but they cannot show him what to think about evident failure. This is perhaps to say that we don't need the religious tradition for morals, but we may need it to teach us what to do about morals.

The religious tradition is therefore paradoxical in its yearning for community. It yearns and yet it remembers that communities are tragic. It has to take into account the stern impassioned stress of a character such as Oliver Cromwell and at the same time, looking at him, take account of the fact that, as he said, he knew how to deny petitions.

The bishops' witness, using the words *vocation* and *trust,* then seems to say to the business manager that she cannot possibly be loyal to each of her beneficiaries, but she must be faithful to all of them. She can be faithful to many but can be loyal only to one. Faithfulness is the virtue (the habit) with which a good person negotiates the demands of each of those who wants her to be loyal. Service to the interests of one beneficiary to the exclusion of the others is faithless; it is corrupt.

One example of this corruption is the current tendency among federal judges and regulators to evade the stresses of faithfulness with a formula or a principle. For example, the principle being suggested by one influential school of thought about corporate-takeover law is that the manager should resolve the stresses of faithfulness by regarding her enterprise as a set of investments which it is her duty to make profitable. The business press is filled with the arguments of those who insist that corporate managers see themselves in this way. There is also some evidence of broad resistance from corporate managers to that concept of management loyalty.

Ultimately, the difficulty in adopting the point of view that sees the corporation primarily as an investment enterprise is that it corrupts even the profit motive itself. That is perhaps what Pastor Neuhaus means when he talks of "the greedy, grasping, wasting ways of a capitalism that destroys memory, tradition and community."[16] It is in consequence (perhaps, as idolatrous, inherently)

---

16. Neuhaus, "Presidential Platitudes," review of *Reagan's America: Innocents at Home,* by Garry Wills, *Wall Street Journal,* 3 February 1987, p. 30.

a liquidation of community. Tim Metz, New York news editor for the *Wall Street Journal,* made that argument in his review of the recently published biography of T. Boone Pickens (16 March 1987): "The book's diagnosis of the disease infecting a good part of industrial America rings true," Mr. Metz said. "But Mr. Pickens's prescription for the ailment doesn't.

"His solution, dramatically underscored in his past takeover moves, is to end waste of assets by wresting them away from incompetent or unresponsive managements and turning them back to the shareholders—through royalty trusts, share repurchases or takeovers.

"In the end . . . that's liquidation. And liquidation is both shortsighted and doubly unjust. It's shortsighted because it summarily eliminates the potential long-term shareholder, and by dismembering corporations, it reduces corporate philanthropy [I would include corporate citizenship], which is one of the social benefits of large corporations. It's unjust because it may reward rather than punish the bad manager . . . and because it often snatches jobs away from those rank-and-file employees who already are among the principal victims of mismanagement."[17]

A more subtle and more pernicious form of corruption of managers is the notion that managing a business is a *profession.* This is a familiar complex of pretenses among those who study medicine and the law as ways of life. It occurs, for example, when a physician sees himself as having been removed from his organic community (communities) and transported into an institution. It is not the activity, the practice, that produces professionalism, nor the commonality that one feels when applying a

---

17. *Business Week* for 22 December 1986 reported the successful revival of A. & P. by its chairman, James Wood, through a system of giving employees power to decide what stores should do and a bonus equal roughly to the profit margin that investors usually expect in a business such as Mr. Wood's. The business world—and, indeed, Mr. Wood himself—tends to explain such successes in terms of sharing profits. It was interesting to me that an affected labor leader was quoted in this case as attributing success to the fact that employees were asked seriously what could be done to save this failing business. "You'd be amazed," the labor leader said, "at the willingness of people to participate when they can say anything without fear of reprisal"—but also, as Mr. Wood's behavior demonstrated, with the assurance that they would be listened to.

difficult skill among colleagues. It is the institution that corrupts the practice, as in the case of the bar associations of the 1880s, which turned the American lawyer from an ethic of responsibility for the common good to an ethic of service to interests, or in the case of the aggregations of power in medicine that turned those professionals from an ethic of patient well-being to an ethic of patient autonomy.

Either sort of corruption—the focus on only one set of interests, or the pretenses of professionalism—turns my hypothetical manager from the community she finds herself in—and this is what raises the common problem, commonly being talked about, of "how to discipline an autonomous, unresponsive management" (Johnson). The spectre offered here, universally implied in any case, is that of a "management class" that labors mainly for the maintenance of its own power. The usual solution in liberal democracies is to turn the management of business over to the government, in about the way associations of workers turned their commonality into a part in the engine of industrial democracy. One way to find that result repulsive is to imagine what the consequences of government control will be (to compare the exchange of organic community among workers for the illusory security and faint promise of influence that has come from government bent on maintenance of production and industrial peace). Another and more theoretical way to find that result repulsive is to remember what an organic community is and to want to preserve such a community or find it or *return* to it, and then to notice that the one thing law in liberal democracy cannot provide in theory, and has not provided in fact, is community.

The test for a communal approach to the law's treatment of corporate management in the takeover wars would be to look for ways in which the law might heighten the moral responsibility of managers, by giving them incentives to maintain business community—incentives that, according to my argument, they already have and want to have. These would be alternatives—alternatives from the religious tradition in the sense I have tried to describe it, alternatives to the forces of professionalism (the management class, including the management class of lawyers and judges) and of social Darwinism (which amounts to the same thing, since social Darwinism works only with coercive guarantees it obtains from the government).

The law has sometimes evidenced a jurisprudence of such incentives. Some of the quainter of these include intrafamilial immunity from civil liability; protection of parental responsibility for education, care, and support of children; and the rescue doctrine in tort. I mention the quaint legal incentives only to show that the law is not hopeless; even lawyers know how to encourage and protect communities—even we remember how. And there are better examples in business and within the takeover context itself: I am thinking of the recent development of the "silver parachute" and similar worker-protection devices in the practice of preventive corporate-takeover law. These operate to assure that workers in an enterprise that is absorbed in the investor wars will keep their human investment or at least will be paid well (as managers and investors are) for having to give it up.[18] These help protect the enterprise as community by making it less attractive to raiders, and they help to strengthen the community by demonstrating that even employees, even in late twentieth-century industrial America, are what Adolph Berle called "stakeholders."

This preventive-law practice does not exclude shareholders. The manager I envision here—the one who knows about communities because she remembers her particular people—seeks, after all, to be faithful. Shareholders have a claim on the faithful manager, but their claim is strongest when it is consonant with claims being made by workers, local communities, and consumers. The fact that the claims of constituencies often coincide is what gives hope to faithfulness and makes community possible; this ordinary, everyday, human fact also shows how morally impoverished it is to divide people, as the law in liberal democracy tends to do, according to interests.

Abraham Chayes once spoke of the people who fall within such a business community as "all those having a relation of sufficient intimacy with the corporation or [being] subject to its

---

18. There are reports of several of these provisions as "shark repellents" adopted in corporate documents, and one or two reports of them as part of agreements for negotiated mergers. They are preventive-law devices, not legislative, and therefore their shape changes all the time. See Thomas J. Murray, "Here Comes the 'Tin' Parachute," *Dun's Business Month*, January 1987, p. 62.

power in a sufficiently specified way." Commonality lies deeper than that; evidence of deeper commonality is the fact that the claims of constituencies within the community often coincide. Those who find evidence of God's purpose in such aggregations of people might say, as Karl Barth did, that God finds us where he put us. This is to see management within a corporation as organic rather than as either a commodity or a profession. It also suggests how we can talk about "corporate purpose" in a way that comprehends the customs and mores and moral judgments that every business person understands when she or he talks about moral behavior in business life.

My son Andy watched with me a recent television news discussion of the current crop of insider trading cases on Wall Street. At one point, Andy asked, with reference to federal law on the subject, "How could you expect that a person whose ethic is profit would obey a rule like that?" How indeed! My hypothetical manager, caught in the winds of takeover, is invited by the evident tendency of American corporate law to decide in favor of short-term wealth maximization for speculator-shareholders. She is seen—by the law—to be a person who cannot bear to think about the burden of character and ambiguity in human enterprise, who must seek in place of such a burden some singular loyalty to guide her behavior. The result of the law's escape in this situation, and perhaps the only way escape is possible, is to turn corporate management over to the state. Arguing against this escape is what I think of as the ordinary tendency of a corporate manager to act as if she is in a community. There would then be no decisive tension between investors and management, although there might be a wariness toward investors who are not in the community and not interested in being in it.[19]

The tendency among some academic commentators is to see the situation as providing a choice—either government control or "the market." But that is not a choice; the market *is* the

---

19. For a moment, the common law allowed corporate managers to make a distinction between speculator-investors and investors who are in the community—see *Unocal Corporation v. Mesa Petroleum Co.*, 493 A.2d 946 (Delaware 1985)—but the federal government quickly preempted that state common-law judgment, and the law now denies the distinction.

government. The choice here—the one a prophet might notice—
is between the law's rejection of the possibility of community in
a business enterprise and its recognition of the yearning for community that comes to the manager because of the community she
comes from. The problem with the law's coercive support of "the
market" (meaning the market in corporate shares, which, when
dominated, gives power to determine who managers are) is that
it rejects community and demands instead a coerced management loyalty to one of many constituencies in the enterprise.
Which is to move the dominance of business enterprise from a
management that is criticized for self-regard to dependence on
the state as a guarantor of fairness.[20] Moses warned the children
of Israel, as they paused on the borders of Canaan, to be wary of
solutions like that, and to remember who they were.[21]

20. I have profited from Lyman Johnson, "Corporate Takeovers
and Corporations: Who Are They For?" *Washington and Lee Law Review*
43 (1986): 781; Christopher X. Axworthy, "Corporation Law as if Some
People Mattered," *University of Toronto Law Journal* 36 (1986): 392;
Robert E. Rodes, Jr., *Law and Liberation* (Notre Dame, Ind.: University of
Notre Dame Press, 1986); and from personal conversation with and advice from Professor Johnson.

21. I have had valuable advice from Frank S. Alexander, Harlan R.
Beckley, Emily Albrink Fowler, Mark H. Grunewald, Stanley Hauerwas,
Andrew W. McThenia, David K. Millon, Brian C. Murchison, Gregory M.
Stanton, Andrew P. Shaffer, Mary M. Shaffer, and John Howard Yoder.

Living without Rights—
In Manners, Religion, and Law

Richard Stith

The rhetoric of rights permeates and dominates American legal thought today. Even ethics is often considered to involve fundamentally a mutual respect for "moral rights." Understanding human rights is taken to be a sufficient condition for knowing how we do and should order our life together.

I disagree. I think that with regard to rights, as to so much else, our modern modes of thought fail fully to capture the ways we still live, and therefore wrongly limit our choices concerning how we should live.

All this is commonplace. With some frequency in the academic literature, it has been noted that our times are peculiarly "rights infatuated."[1] And with similar frequency, this fact has been lamented.[2] There are many who do not agree that

---

1. See R. B. Louden, "Rights Infatuation and the Impoverishment of Moral Theory," *Journal of Value Inquiry* 17 (1983): 87-102. Among the best, albeit short, histories of the modern idea of rights are John Finnis's *Natural Law and Natural Rights* (Oxford: Clarendon Press, 1980), pp. 205-10; and M. P. Golding's "The Concept of Rights: A Historical Sketch," in *Bioethics and Human Rights,* ed. E. L. Bandman and B. Bandman (Boston: Little, Brown, 1978), pp. 44-50. See also Golding's more refined treatment "Justice and Rights: A Study in Relationship," in *Justice and Health Care,* ed. E. E. Shelp (Boston: D. Reidel, 1981), pp. 23-35.

2. See, for example, Louden, "Rights Infatuation and the Im-

rights alone can provide an adequate basis for human community.

But recent analyses have been able to show only that significant normative values lie outside some sphere of immediate individual relationships which must still be relegated to rights.[3] I want to point out something more: that our practices reveal alternatives to rights even within that sphere. I think I have found something not only in addition to rights but also instead of rights. Some rights can and ought to be rejected in favor of what I call "duties of generosity."

The practices to which I turn first for non-rights-based relations are part neither of morals nor of law, however. They belong to what is called "manners" or "courtesy" or, more descriptively, "graciousness."[4] After considering at length polite practices of mutual generosity that cannot be described in terms of rights, we shall look briefly at Christian religious tradition for analogues. Martin Luther and William of Ockham will help us to understand what it might mean to expand these duties of graciousness throughout the political and even the cosmic worlds. Last of all we shall ponder whether and how to conserve or to change modern civil law itself, so that it might best lead us to live more generously together.

---

poverishment of Moral Theory"; Theodore Benditt, *Rights* (Totowa, N.J.: Rowman & Littlefield, 1982); Karl Marx, "On the Jewish Question," in *Early Writings* (New York: Random House, 1975), pp. 230-31; J. Narveson, commentary on Feinberg's essay "The Nature and Value of Rights," *Journal of Value Inquiry* 4 (1970): 258-60; Law and Ecological Ethics Symposium, *Osgood Hall Law Journal* 22 (1984): 281-348; J. Raz, "Right-Based Moralities," in *Utility and Rights,* ed. R. G. Frey (Minneapolis: University of Minnesota Press, 1984), pp. 42-59; Michael Sandal, *Liberalism and the Limits of Justice* (New York: Cambridge University Press, 1982); and Ch. Taylor, "Atomism," in *Powers, Possessions and Freedom: Essays in Honour of C. B. Macpherson,* ed. A. Kontos (Toronto: University of Toronto, 1979), pp. 39-61.

3. See especially works cited in notes 7-10 herein.

4. So far as I have been able to determine, recent normative theory has been curiously uninterested in the structure of modern manners, as opposed to that of modern morals or of modern law. Ronald Dworkin has used "philosophy of courtesy" as a foil (see *Law's Empire* [London: Fontana Press, 1986], pp. 45-86), but I know of no one who has seriously taken up this task.

DO DUTIES IMPLY RIGHTS?

One conceptually clear way to understand the limitations of rights begins with the commonly held "correlativity thesis." This thesis is that for every right there exists a correlative duty and that for every duty there exists a correlative right.[5] For example, if A has a duty to pay a debt to B, it is said to follow necessarily that B has a right to be paid by A. And likewise wherever B has such a right, A has such a duty.[6] "Such" is an important word here, because the correlativity thesis applies only to rights that are *claims* against another, not to rights that are merely *liberties*. A may well have a liberty right to run his competitor B out of business without B having any duty to close up shop.

Perhaps the existence of liberty rights could be said to weaken the correlativity thesis, in that certain significant rights are thus shown not to correspond to anyone else's duty. But, for our purposes here, the wrong side of the thesis is weakened. We are interested not in whether there is a duty for every right but in whether there is a right for every duty.

Why so? Well, if there is a right for every duty, then it follows that the set of rights is equal to or greater than the set of duties. If every duty implies a right, then the modern primacy of

---

5. Alan White, for example, asserts the commonness of this view, though he does not himself share it (see *Rights* [Oxford: Clarendon Press, 1984], p. 85). Those who have proposed the thesis appear to include S. I. Benn and R. S. Peters, *The Principles of Political Thought* (New York: Free Press, 1959), pp. 102, 107; and Charles Fried, *Right and Wrong* (Cambridge: Harvard University Press, 1978), p. 81. John Finnis seems implicitly to hold such a view when he states "The concept of rights is not . . . of less importance or dignity [than the concept of duties]: for the common good is precisely the good of those individuals whose *benefit,* from fulfillment of duty by others, is their *right* because *required* of those others in justice" (*Natural Law and Natural Rights,* p. 210 n. 1). See also Carleton Kemp Allen, *Legal Duties* (Oxford: Clarendon Press, 1931), pp. 156-220; R. W. M. Dias, *Jurisprudence,* 4th ed. (London: Butterworth's, 1976), pp. 36-39; and George Whitcross Paton, *A Textbook of Jurisprudence* (Oxford: Clarendon Press, 1972), p. 285. Other philosophers have denied the second half of the thesis, as explained later in the text.

6. This analysis of correlativity is, of course, that of Wesley N. Hohfeld, *Fundamental Legal Conceptions* (New Haven: Yale University Press, 1919).

rights talk is justified. Rights analysis covers the normative universe in that it ends up describing all rights and all duties according to this side of the correlativity thesis. On the other hand, if some duties do not imply rights, then thinking about rights must be supplemented by thinking about duties if some of the latter are not to be overlooked. The adequacy of rights-based thinking is, therefore, appropriately attacked by pointing to duties that do not correspond to rights.[7]

Many scholars have, in fact, sought to discredit the thesis that every duty of one individual implies a right in some other individual by pointing to apparently rightless duties. It is said, for example, that alleged duties to oneself cannot correspond to rights. Again, it has been argued that duties to God or to the state are not perfectly captured by rights language suitable for other human individuals.[8] Likewise, it is contended that many of our duties are to classes rather than to individuals and that therefore no one can be said to have correlative rights. I may have a duty to give to the poor, but no particular beggar has a right to my money.[9]

---

7. Benditt (in *Rights*), Louden (in "Rights Infatuation and the Impoverishment of Moral Theory"), and Raz (in "Right-Based Moralities") all point out that we may well have rights that we ought not to exercise. This "ought" is something else that rights talk misses. I do not mean to deny or minimize this important critique of rights, but it is not germane to this part of my analysis. It is a critique as much of the *must do*'s of duties as of the *must have*'s of rights, for it points out that both duties and rights may miss the more subtle *oughts* and *shoulds* of human relationships. My first interest here is to demonstrate that rights are inadequate even to convey all the strong and clear imperatives of duty.

8. John Austin calls these rightless duties "absolute" (*Lectures on Jurisprudence*, vol. 2 [New York: Burt Franklin, 1861], pp. 66-75; cf. the critiques by Allen in *Legal Duties* and by Paton in *A Textbook of Jurisprudence*.

9. Besides Austin, *Lectures on Jurisprudence*, and Benditt, *Rights*, see John Stuart Mill, *Utilitarianism*, ed. H. B. Acton (London: J. M. Dent, 1972), pp. 46-47. Joel Feinberg mentions these "duties of charity" in *Rights, Justice, and the Bounds of Liberty* (Princeton University Press, 1980), pp. 135-39, 144.

Feinberg also refers obscurely to rightless "duties of self-sacrifice," citing as examples acts of heroism mentioned by H. B. Acton, "Symposium on 'Rights,'" *Proceedings of the Aristotelian Society*, Supplementary Vol. 24 (1950): 107-8. Feinberg, Acton, and Benditt may be calling at-

But not one of these arguments, whatever their merits may be, points to situations in which I have a duty to benefit a particular human being without that person having a right against me. These arguments thus appear to concede that our duties to benefit other human individuals are fully described in terms of rights. Yet it is just this implicit concession that I refuse. I want to discover ways to hold onto neighborly duties without invoking neighborly rights.

Some readers may fault me here for having failed to mention the many "will-based" theories of rights, which make the existence of rightless duties to individuals obvious.[10] Not every particular beneficiary of someone else's duty is a rightholder, so these theories contend, for in order to have a right one must have a choice. Someone's duty to give me a steer does not per se imply that I have a property or a contract right to it. I have this right only if I have some remedy I can use effectively to obtain the steer if it is withheld, or perhaps also unless I have the ability to waive (or even to transfer) a claim to it. Such choices are not open to me, under English law for example, where I am a third-party beneficiary of a contract between my father and a rancher or where the state has simply commanded the cattleman to redistribute his wealth under pain of criminal punishment. Criminal law duties, according to these theories, often impose duties on individuals without granting rights to other persons. Although you have a duty not to kill me, I have no full right not to be killed by you, because I cannot make the state provide me

---

tention to duties without rights similar to those discussed in this essay, but their duties of heroic self-sacrifice are unlike the ones I discuss below in that theirs are far more rare than mine. Moreover, at least some of theirs might be construed as duties without rights only because of a confused juxtaposition of two different subjective points of view. A hero may feel under a duty while his beneficiaries do not feel a right to his services. But within his own subjective world, a hero might well say that those who are aided have "a right" to his help even if they do not realize it. Finally, none of these writers draws attention to the mutuality of rightless duties which is my focus here.

10. H. L. A. Hart is the leading figure here; see his essay "Bentham on Legal Rights," in *Rights,* ed. D. Lyons (Belmont, Cal.: Wadsworth, 1979), pp. 125-48. See also Allen, *Legal Duties;* Dias, *Jurisprudence;* Finnis, *Natural Law and Natural Rights;* Golding, "Justice and Rights"; and Paton, *A Textbook of Jurisprudence.*

with police protection, nor can I or my estate force the state to punish an unsuccessful or successful attempt to murder me. And, of course, I cannot sell my right to life to some rich sadist in exchange for some preferred benefit to my family. Similarly, according to some theories, duties to infants and to the very senile (not to mention to fetuses and to animals) cannot involve rights, because the beneficiaries of said duties are presently physically unable to exercise rational choice.[11]

A moment's reflection will show, however, that this method of demonstrating the existence of duties without rights is not what we are seeking. It does not look for unnoticed duties that the catalogue of rights has missed. It simply takes the list of claim rights and shortens it. Will-based rights theory shows at most that a narrow definition of rights will not adequately bring to light all duties. It does not show that the commonsense notion of rights as legally or morally required benefits (which notion holds that both I and an infant have a right to life) is not sufficient. But it is this latter, popular notion that permits rights talk to dominate our thought, and so it is this that must be shown to give an inadequate account of duties.

Nor have benefit-based theories of rights surrendered entirely to will-based theories in the academic world, though they have been refined in response to some of the arguments we have already noted.[12] A leading advocate of the benefit theory of rights has recently claimed that being a "direct, intended" beneficiary of a duty is sufficient for having a right.[13] It is these of this sort that I shall oppose, not by redefining rights more narrowly but by calling attention to duties directly to benefit other individuals that cannot be translated into *anyone's* language of rights. In so doing, I will be attacking the very core of correlativity and presenting the possibility of the rejection of rights in human relationships founded on duty.

---

11. See, for example, P. Montague, "Two Concepts of Rights," *Philosophy and Public Affairs* 9 (1980): 372, 384.

12. See, for example, the telling response to Hart by Neil MacCormick in "Rights in Legislation," in *Law, Morality, and Society*, ed. P. M. S. Hacker and J. Raz (Oxford: Oxford University Press, 1977), pp. 189, 198.

13. David Lyons, *Rights*, pp. 63, 73. I am referring to duties to benefit specific other persons, not to so-called "useful duties."

SOME DUTIES OF MUTUAL GENEROSITY

Consider the following commonly accepted social rule for tea parties and the like: "No one may take the last cookie." Translated into our terms here, the rule becomes "Everyone has a duty to leave the last cookie." There is a mutual duty to leave the last cookie uneaten.[14]

Although I shall appeal a bit to our shared beliefs and practices in analyzing this rule, my primary purpose is not anthropological but logical. Even someone unfamiliar with this rule or someone who disagreed with my more detailed description of it ought to concede that the duty I depict is a possible one. That concession is all I need in order to show that we may have duties intended directly to benefit others that do not correspond to rights possessed by those others.

Can this cookie-leaving duty be translated into the language of rights, as the correlativity thesis would demand? Certainly it cannot without contradiction be straightforwardly transformed into a statement of individual claim rights. The rule "Everyone has a right to take the last cookie" is self-contradictory, if by it we mean that every person both has a binding claim in his or her favor and also has equally binding claims in opposition. Or, put another way, our normative practices do not permit us coherently to assert that A has a valid claim to the cookie, while B, C, and the rest also have identically valid claims. Rights in a

---

14. Some readers may object that the term *duty* seems too strong here. I have two responses. The first is that our language permits the word *duty* to designate all behavior mandated by a nonoptional social institution. Only so long as an institution is felt to be optional does the word *duty* seem excessive. For example, it strikes us as odd to say that a man has a duty to dance with a woman, but a dancing instructor of young people might well say "A gentleman has a duty to ask a lady sitting by herself to dance," because he and his audience are at that time committed to the conventions of social dance. Similarly, if we consider the breach of proper cookie behavior to be unthinkable, the word *duty* seems appropriate. My second response is that nothing turns on the word *duty* anyway. My point is not to rank such behavior high or low, in a normative hierarchy, but to discern its inner logic. I want to ask whether and when sentences in the imperative form referred to by the word *duty* entail correlative rights. I have chosen the word solely for this purpose, not for its connotations or as part of any wider axiological assertion.

conclusory or absolute sense must be exclusive, but any lesser degree of rights would not adequately represent the unequivocal duties of our original formulation. Moreover, even reducing the rights involved to nonabsolutely weighted interests would not eliminate the antinomy, for even these lesser claims, being all identical, are incapable of leading to a resolution of the problem of what to do with the cookie. No one can eat the cookie without violating many other equal rights. Yet to leave it on the table would be worst of all, for only this solution would violate *everyone's* rights. By contrast, there is no contradiction nor even any slight tension in the original duty formulation. The result is never in doubt. If everyone abides by his or her duty, the cookie simply remains uncontested and uneaten.

Even if we try to restate our duties merely as liberty rights (rather than as claim rights), we are unsuccessful. If everyone had a liberty right to the cookie, it is true that all could, without logical or normative difficulty, make a grab for it. The fastest or strongest would eat it, and no one else could claim that his or her rights had been violated. But everyone who made such an effort would have violated (or at least attempted to violate) the duty not to take the cookie. To be at liberty means, by definition, that one is under no duty, so liberty rights obviously cannot express a situation where everyone is under a duty.

In addition, one's supposed cookie claim right could not be exercised without violating one's duty, so that yet another contradiction in a claim rights translation has been shown. One cannot have a right to do that which one has a duty not to do — where, as here, the duties and rights in question operate on the same level within the same institution. (It is possible to say, for example, that one has a legal right to do X but a *moral* duty not to do X. But one cannot say that one has a legal right to do X and also a *legal* duty not to do X.) Rendering mutual duties not to take the cookie as mutual claim rights to the cookie brings about insoluble antinomies both among rights and between rights and duties.

There is, however, one rights formulation that at first glance appears adequately to express everyone's duty to leave the cookie alone: "Everyone has the right to have no one else eat the cookie"—that is, to have the cookie go to waste. Under this latter formulation, no one could claim the last cookie, but each could

feel properly aggrieved and could rightfully complain if someone else took the cookie. I must agree that this translation is not
self-contradictory in any way, nor does it contradict the original
duty rule. But to state it is to reveal the incompleteness of our
original rule statement. Those who practice the duty rule would
surely also find it most impolite and ungracious for anyone
seriously to complain when someone else ate the cookie. So let
us temporarily reformulate the original rule as follows: "Everyone
has a duty to leave the last cookie *and not to object if someone else
takes it.*"

Furthermore, the proposed translation of the duty to leave
the cookie into the right to see that the cookie goes to waste
seems to miss the intent of those who do their duty. The intent
is to have someone else eat the cookie, not to have it left over.
The whole point of rule compliance here, as it might be explained
to a child learning it, is generously to grant other people's appetites precedence over one's own. To complain when one's wish
is fulfilled would be to contradict that intent. We can thus com-
bine the idea of noncomplaint and that of the intended beneficiary
into a simpler and final duty formulation: "Everyone has a duty
to leave the last cookie *for someone else.*"[15]

Is it possible, however, that this duty to let others eat the
cookie is but the indirect reflection of some other duty, which
might possibly be expressed in terms of rights? For example, it
has been suggested to me that the duty here might really be to
the host: guests might leave the last cookie in order to keep the
host from worrying that he or she had not provided enough
food.[16] This attractive idea, however, is open to several objections. For one thing, even if such a duty to the host exists, it does
not correspond to any host rights. It would be absurd for a host
to insist that no one eat the last cookie so that he or she could

---

15. One could adduce less rich examples where the impossibility
of waste as a goal would be still more obvious. Consider what happens
when two similarly situated persons reach a closed door simultaneously. Each has a duty to open and hold the door for the other, while neither
has a right to have the door held open. It cannot be that the purpose of
this mutual duty is to have the benefit of first entry go to waste—that
is, to have each refuse to go through the door until the other has done
so, leaving both permanently outside.

16. The suggestion was made by Professor James Albers.

imagine all to be satisfied. Furthermore, the duty-to-the-host idea does not fully capture the practice we have already described. If the host were the real intended beneficiary, then surely it would be within the rights, and even the duties, of each guest tactfully to stop others from eating the cookie. But this is not done.

Moreover, if by some chance all other persons have left the room without eating the cookie, I know of no rule still forbidding one to eat the cookie. Similarly, it is common (though quite difficult because politeness discourages candor) to attempt to determine whether in fact anyone else present really wants the cookie. If no one else does, then one is free to eat it. This fact shows that others as intended beneficiaries are absolutely essential to the original rule. When they are absent, or when they are already satisfied and so cannot benefit, the rule has no application. Therefore, the rule does not aim at waste or at pleasing a host. Even when rule compliance makes the cookie go uneaten, it remains on the table as a symbol of our mutual care for one another.[17]

Nor, let it be emphasized, is the duty an ascetic one, meant to combat self-indulgent gluttony or to encourage self-sacrifice for its own sake, for, if it were, it would remain in force when one were alone as well as among others.

We have discovered, then, a duty directly to benefit other individuals which cannot be translated into rights, no matter how rights may be defined. What name should be given to this newly discovered creature? "Graciousness" seems almost correct, but a bit too broad and too connotative of style rather than of substance. "Deference" may be too small spirited. While I own that the title is not perfect, I would contend that the mutual duty we have unearthed is appropriately called one of "generosity," because it involves an obligation to relinquish potential possession to someone who has no right to possession. And it involves a *duty*, rather than a supererogatory act of generosity, because one does wrong in taking the cookie for oneself.

That last description of the beneficiary of this duty is not quite complete, however. Someone who takes the last cookie when others might want it not only has no right to possess it but also violates a duty to leave the cookie for others. Yet others at

---

17. I owe this felicitous expression to my secretary Pat McRae.

the table not only should not object, but should be pleased—since the cookie is being consumed by an intended beneficiary.

Notice how strange this intended beneficiary has become: the last cookie is left precisely for someone who does not do his or her duty. Our duty is to leave the cookie for someone whose appetite is so imperious that duty's command is ignored. This mutual duty of generosity is a duty to benefit those who do wrong. Such duties are nearly unheard of in legal and moral systems, but they abound in manners and in religion.

Consider, for example, the following: "A host has a duty to provide as many towels as a guest might desire. A guest has a duty not to request any towels which a host might desire." Here we are dealing no longer with identical duties incumbent upon all participants in a practice of graciousness. (The guest has no duty to provide towels for the host.) The prior example envisioned only one role (that of potential cookie eater), while here there are two (those of host and of guest). It is important briefly to consider this variation on mutual duties of generosity, since it would seem to be rather more common. Complementary duties are more numerous than identical duties in human interactions.

The problem in essence is the same, however. Just as we previously wondered what to do with a mutually wanted cookie, here we ask ourselves, as host or as guest, what should be done with mutually desired towels. And the answer, as a matter of duty, is equally clear: the towels should be left for the other, who (if he or she in fact retains or obtains the coveted towels) is violating a duty.

Can these duties be coherently translated into rights? No, for the same reasons we have already explored. A guest cannot have a right to towels desired by a host and the host at the same time have a right to towels desired by the guest. Such a translation incoherently pits one's rights against another's rights and against one's own duties. Yet from duties there results no contradiction, and we do find our way to a clear if rough solution: the host should provide as large a pile of towels as a guest could possibly wish, even to the point of skipping his or her own bath if towels are scarce, while a guest who suspects such a scarcity should take few if any towels from the pile (insofar as, but no further than, the guest has reason to hope that the towels left behind might end up being used by the host).

A variant practice also exists: the original towel possessor (the host) offers additional towels to a bath-hungry guest who graciously refuses to take them. The host then "insists" and the guest continues to refuse until one or the other gives in. This resolution occurs either because one has been convinced that the other truly does not desire the towels or because one has breached the duty to be towelless. (It is also possible that the towels have been retained not out of a desire for towels but rather out of a desire to respect the other's sense of duty to relinquish them, of which more later.) This variant has the obvious advantage that the towels do not go to waste, but it does not involve any essential alteration of duties.

Note that this practice, again, does not demand self-sacrifice for its own sake. It is perfectly all right not to offer towels (and also all right to request and use towels) that the other person cannot possibly desire—which is not to deny that at some point an additional duty not to be gluttonous or ungrateful might come into play to limit absolutely the number of towels one should hoard.

There seems little point in multiplying examples further. Courtesy duties of generosity are so common and important to our life together that I would suppose they take more instructional time than do morals in educating the next generation, perhaps precisely because young children find it hard to grasp the fundamental point that such duties are not to be translated into rights. A child, in my experience, immediately converts the duty to let others play with the toys in his or her possession into a right to play with toys possessed by others. Indignant outrage follows, and must continue to follow, such a translation—because in terms of rights this rule is self-contradictory. Only when the mutual duty of generosity has been grasped can there be peace (which may not occur until toys become no more important than towels in the child's life).

A THEORY OF GENEROSITY DUTIES

The special character of mutual duties of generosity, and its distinction from that of rights, can be further brought out by a real property metaphor.

The phenomenology, the *feel*, of a right is that of a rule-protected power or control (insofar as one has secured that to which one has a right) and of a rule-supported claiming or demanding such power (insofar as one is not yet in possession of that to which one has a right). As spheres of potentially absolute and arbitrary power, rights are litigious by nature, one might say, so that there can be no peace as long as rights seem to overlap or, a fortiori, as long as they actually do overlap (as in the translations of cookie, towel, and toy duties). A normative system of rights requires *exactitude*. There must be precise and known boundary lines between Whiteacre and Blackacre if incoherence and squabbling are to be avoided.

By contrast, mutual duties of generosity involve "buffer zones" extending back a bit from the boundaries to which rights would press. Each property owner has a duty to relinquish the use of these zones to the other. That is, each has a duty both not to use the buffer strip and also not to object to the use of the strip by the neighbor. The result is that litigation is lessened. Trespass does not trigger conflict. Minor infractions of duty are accepted, and even welcomed in the best of all worlds. Only major intrusions are brought to court (just as there might properly be objections if someone ate *all* the cookies).

It is essential to ask here whether property still exists in a practical sense in the buffer zones. That is, is there any difference (from the point of view, say, of the owner of Whiteacre) between the yardage the frontier zone intrudes into Whiteacre and the yardage it intrudes into Blackacre? I think not, though from a certain formal point of view the first remains the "property" of the owner of Whiteacre, while the second remains alien. Similarly, the cookie duties and the towel duties were not significantly different, despite the fact that, by hypothesis, the last cookie was the property of none of the potential eaters, while the towels were the property of the host. What we have along the border is, therefore, a realm without property *or* rights, a realm of what one might call "lawless altruism."

We may observe in passing that private property is thus not necessary to generosity, a conclusion frequently disputed.[18] When-

---

18. Feinberg puts it this way: "consciousness of one's rights is *necessary* for the supererogatory virtues, for the latter cannot even be given a sense except by contrast with the disposition always to claim one's rights" (*Rights, Justice, and the Bounds of Liberty*, p. 157).

ever one, without being coerced, relinquishes de facto possession of a good to someone who does not have a right to possession, one is being generous. This statement remains true even if one is under a duty so to act, as we have seen. Note that it is not essential that one be giving up one's own property. Generosity is possible even among thieves and even in a Hobbesian state of nature. And from the point of view of the recipient who had no right to what he or she obtained (and may even have had a duty to refuse it), gratitude is called for.

Is a world without property, a world of "lawless altruism," any more stable or desirable than one of "lawless egoism"? The simple answer is that two people can sacrifice the same object more easily than two can acquire the same object. As long as we are willing to put up with waste, or willing to see the buffer not as waste but as a symbol of mutual regard, peace would seem to ensue. However, it must be admitted that in the most gracious of all worlds, each side would actually plead with the other to use the entire zone (the "I insist" we noted before), and the other side would wish to use the zone not in order to obtain some personal gain but in order to please his or her altruistic neighbor. Since both sides would feel the same, at each level and ad infinitum, a kind of good-natured "battle" might occur. A dialectical synthesis might be found in which *both* sides could come to sacrifice themselves for the other: the one by deferring to the other's territorial desires and the latter by occupying the territory in deference to the former's desire to be dutiful. The first sacrifices land, and the second sacrifices virtue.

Even the defects of such a system constitute a strength. Waste or a battle over generosity is in fact not likely to occur, because people are not going to be wholly duty-minded, and the system has anticipated this fact. Minor violations of duty are expected and promote efficiency, while extreme violations are checked by rights as well as by conscience. "Lawless altruism" is, therefore, clearly preferable to "lawless egoism."

In all my analysis so far, I have presumed mutual identical or complementary duties. Indeed, it is the fact of mutuality that has enabled us to establish that duties can exist without correlative rights. Can this presupposition be removed? Can one have duties of generosity toward those who have neither rights nor duties toward one? I do not see why not. If I can dutifully leave a cookie for a rational adult who ought to do the same for me, why can I not leave a cookie for a small child not yet subject to duties? If the rational adult has no right to the cookie, why need the child have a right? I think that nothing requires the child to have any right (or at least any claim right) to the cookie, though no wrong is done when the child eats it.

The reason we began with mutual duties is that the benefit theory of rights could otherwise easily have argued that a duty to another person must by definition, as it were, involve a right on the part of that person. We can now see that this is not the case. To say the child has a right to the cookie *adds* something, phenomenologically, to the statement that I have a duty to let the child have the cookie. Specifically, it adds an imaginary or real claim of power over the cookie on the part of the child, a vain or effective appeal to rules to force me to give the cookie. *The language of rights militantly reduces rules from an object of common loyalty to the status of security guards at the beck and call of the right-holder.* And I am likewise reduced from a servant of the law to a servant of the rightholder. This phenomenological reflection shows, by the way, that will-based theories are nearer than benefit-based theories to the essence of rights. Rights always involve self-centered (which may not be equivalent to "selfish") acts of will, at least in the imagination. A duty not to make such an appeal is perhaps the easiest and most effective way to prevent a rights consciousness from arising, but it is not strictly necessary. It is necessary only that no reductionistic appeal by the beneficiary be imagined or realized.

Joel Feinberg has used the language of aristocracy to call a world without rights—even one in which most people conscientiously do their duties—"servile."[19] Property and rights are needed, he would seem to be saying, in order to promote human dignity. But do our experiences in this rightless realm of graciousness bear him out? I think not. Rights subject us to each other, while duties subject us only to a common law. One might say that rights convert the law itself into something that can in part be privately owned. Rights, not duties, are the baser way to order our life together. To be generous and self-sacrificing on the one hand, and gratefully to accept benefits recogniz-

---

19. Feinberg, *Rights, Justice, and the Bounds of Liberty*, p. 156.

ing that one does not have a right to them on the other, is the more noble life.

A final touch should be added to this sketch of duties of generosity. Note that no mention has yet been made of the inculcation of the virtue of generosity nor of the enforcement of the duties pertaining thereto. The simple reason for this omission is that our purpose has been normative and logical, not genetic. How to bring about and maintain generous ways of living together is an empirical and psychological question separate from the question of how to describe the inner logic of a system of duties without rights.

But mention should be made here of the peculiar logical irrelevance of enforcement mechanisms to the system that has been described. Neither party to a cookie dispute has any rational self-interest (other than pure envy) in violating the duty of noncomplaint by appealing to higher powers. If such powers were to step in, it could only be to remind *all* parties that *none* may have the cookie—not to allocate the cookie to anyone. This is what children finally learn after many futile attempts to make parents enforce their rights to toys.

Note, too, that even the intervention of higher enforcement authority does not re-create the exactitude of a system of rights. An enforcing power would require *both* property owners to move back from the buffer zone. It would not be interested in the erection or protection of a boundary fence (except insofar as this might be required for the definition of the buffer zone). The duty-enforcing state or community is not interested in total and exact control of the world, in deciding precisely who eats the cookie or farms the land. The realm we have discovered is not simply one in which individuals are duty-bound to submit to injustice, while a higher ideal of justice remains available and perhaps enforceable by God or by a civil authority. *There is no just allocation* of the cookie or the towels or the toys or the borderland. There is no "right" answer. There is only the possibility of possessing and the duty not to do so.

DOES RELIGION RADICALIZE THESE DUTIES?

Similarities between the small-scale duties of self-sacrifice so far described and the more extensive commands of the Christian gospel cannot have passed unnoticed. Let us look more closely at this apparent congruence, for it may reveal the possibilities or limits of last-cookie relationships.

An absolute extension of the cookie model is not difficult to conceive abstractly. Each human being would have a duty generously to give up any part of himself or herself—be it possessions, liberty, or life—that might be desired by someone else. Others would have identical or complementary duties. Not only would the ideas of rights and property not exist but even the idea of justice would have no meaning. All distributions of mutually desired goods would be equally appropriate and inappropriate. In the absence of an abundance so great that all persons could be satisfied, only waste or endless generosity battles would be called for—though in fact we could presume that self-interest would result in possession and consumption (limited to some degree by conscience and by power).

Does Christianity demand such a world? In his 1523 essay "Temporal Authority: To What Extent It Should Be Obeyed," Luther at first glance appears to be fully as radical as our model would require. He begins with the Scriptures:

> Christ says in Matthew 5[:38-41], "You have heard that it was said to them of old: An eye for an eye, a tooth for a tooth. But I say to you, Do not resist evil; but if anyone strikes you on the right cheek, turn to him the other also. And if anyone would sue you and take your coat, let him have your cloak as well. And if anyone forces you to go one mile, go with him two miles," etc. Likewise Paul in Romans 12[:19], "Beloved, defend not yourselves, but leave it to the wrath of God; for it is written, 'Vengeance is mine; I will repay, says the Lord.'" And in Matthew 5[:44], "Love your enemies, do good to them that hate you." And again, in I Peter 2[3:9], "Do not return evil for evil, or reviling for reviling," etc. . . . Be certain too that this teaching of Christ is not a counsel for those who would be perfect, as our sophists blasphemously and falsely say, but a universally obligatory command for all Christians. Then you will realize that all those who avenge themselves or go to law and wrangle in the courts over their property and honor are nothing but heathen masquerading under the name of Christians. It cannot be otherwise, I tell you. Do not be dissuaded by the multitude and common practice; for there

are few Christians on earth—have no doubt about it—and
God's Word is something very different from the common
practice.[20]

In short, Christians are duty-bound to see "that they do evil to
no one and willingly endure evil at the hands of others."[21] What
is this if not a radicalization of our duty of generosity into an absolute duty to sacrifice ourselves to others' desires, in total dis-
regard of ordinary notions of justice?

Luther does not really go so far. The word *evil* in the last
quotation indeed shows that for him there remains some standard of justice (or at least some standard of good and evil) besides compliance with the duty of self-sacrifice. And this standard becomes the actual object of enforcement for Luther when
the interests of *others* are at stake:

> The true meaning of Christ's words in Matthew 5[:39], "Do
> not resist evil," etc. . . . is this: A Christian should be so dis-
> posed that he will suffer every evil and injustice without
> avenging himself; neither will he seek legal redress in the
> courts but have utterly no need of temporal authority and
> law for his own sake. On behalf of others, however, he may
> and should seek vengeance, justice, protection, and help,
> and do as much as he can to achieve it. Likewise, the
> governing authority should, on its own initiative or
> through the instigation of others, help and protect him too,
> without any complaint, application, or instigation on his
> own part.[22]

Luther, then, seems necessarily to retain some notion of just allocation of goods that it is "evil" to disturb and that the Christian
individually and through the state has a duty to restore whenever the interests of others are at stake. Luther must, in other
words, be willing to distinguish between the *proper needs* of others
and their mere *desires*. The protection of the former takes priority

---

20. *Luther's Works*, vol. 45, ed. W. I. Brandt and H. T. Lehman, rev.
W. I. Brandt, trans. J. J. Schindel (Philadelphia: Muhlenberg Press, 1962),
pp. 87, 101-2.

21. *Luther's Works*, 45:92. Luther later adds the important proviso
that such deference may not contravene divine law, such as the Ten
Commandments (45:111-12). But this limitation is not ordinarily applicable for Luther.

22. *Luther's Works*, 45:101.

over deference to the latter. His vision is not one of a radical absence of justice and property but of a willingness to give up one's own claims while enforcing the just claims of others.

Nevertheless, Luther has achieved a striking reduction in rights consciousness. He has succeeded in separating will rights and benefit rights. He has cut out the self-centered core of rights. We as Christians must struggle to give to others that which is their due. In this duty we certainly have no will right, for there is no option for self involved. We must simply make sure everyone except ourselves gets his or her share of cookies. Others retain benefit rights, but the absense of will rights changes the character even of benefit rights. Because others are also under a duty to sacrifice and not to appeal to the rules to protect themselves, we can no longer even imagine them to be making "self-righteous" claims to the cookies. We thus can secure to others that which is just for them to have without assuming them to have self-centered rights of any sort thereto.

In a sense, what Luther has done is both utterly modern and utterly antimodern. He has separated off from justice the self-centered power to will that is at the core of modernity—but he has done so only in order to reject it. He has taken what amounts to our contemporary concept of "standing to sue," which means having one's own interests at stake, and has made that the single situation in which one may *not* ask that justice be done. When we do ask that justice be enforced, as I have just argued, we need not imagine an imperious power claim on the part of those we are seeking to benefit. We need not think in terms of rights at all. We remain not under men but under God and the law.

And, in an act of dialectic, Luther holds out to us a further hope:

> You may ask, "Why may I not use the sword for myself and for my own cause, so long as it is my intention not to seek my own advantage but to punish evil?" Answer: Such a miracle is not impossible, but very rare and hazardous. Where the Spirit is so richly present it may well happen. For we read thus of Samson in Judges 15[:11], that he said, "As they did to me, so have I done to them." . . . Samson was called of God to harass the Philistines and deliver the children of Israel. Although he used them as an occasion to further his own cause, still he did not do so in order to

> avenge himself or to seek his own interests, but to serve others and to punish the Philistines [Judg. 14:4].[23]

In other words, Luther allows the promotion of justice even for oneself as long as one is not (primarily?) seeking one's own interests. A mother, for example, could be under a duty to make claims for herself on behalf of her children. (We might today call this an assertion of "parental rights," but in so doing we would evoke a different image.) Clearly there is great room for hypocrisy here, but the possibility exists for Luther that justice might become a *common* project, pursued neither for oneself nor against oneself but with indifference to oneself. No longer would the moral and legal worlds be envisioned as matters of competition and allocation among private wills. Doing justice would be promoting that which is right, not securing individual rights.[24]

The great drama Luther describes, then, is indeed related to the more petty interactions that have been our concern in this essay. Both offer ways in which the domination of rights might be resisted. But the ways are somewhat different, and Luther's writings do not encourage us to press our antinomian duties of generosity beyond the borders of human relationships where we originally discovered them.

Luther, of course, did not attempt to use words with juridical precision. And it is I who have imposed the word *rights* upon Luther's thoughts here. But there is someone else who had already attempted a legalistic refinement of a system very similar

---

23. *Luther's Works,* 45:104. Luther's radical heirs continue to struggle to discern the fine line drawn here by Scripture. See for example *The Use of the Law: A Summary Statement Adopted by the Mennonite Church General Assembly, August 11-15, 1981* (Scottdale, Pa.: Mennonite Publishing House, 1982).

24. For reflections on the relative unimportance of rights in a solidaristic community of shared values under an activist state, see M. Damaska, *The Faces of Justice and State Authority* (New Haven: Yale University Press, 1986), especially pp. 83-84. See also my comments in "A Critique of Abortion Rights," *Democracy* 3 (Fall 1983): 60-70; and "New Constitutional and Penal Theory in Spanish Abortion Law," *American Journal of Comparative Law* 35 (Summer 1987). Are there ways to avoid the ruthlessness of valuing (with its common callousness toward particulars) as well as the selfishness of rights? For an affirmative answer, see my essay "Toward Freedom from Value," *The Jurist* 38 (1978): 48-81.

to that of Luther: the nominalist philosopher William of Ockham (ca. 1285-1349).

As a Franciscan, Ockham was faced with the difficult task of justifying the order's use of material goods despite its vow of corporate and individual poverty. An earlier solution, declaring the pope to be the true owner of the property which the friars merely used, had broken down under John XXII—who wished to force the would-be radical order to acknowledge the impossibility of life without property.

According to the philosopher-historian Michel Villey, Ockham's response for the first time defined the idea of "rights" in a way we would recognize today, but did so only in order to permit the Franciscans to reject them.[25] A right *(jus)* for Ockham is a power *(potestas)* over a good that civil law vindicates. That is, one has a right to some good if, when one is deprived of power over the good without one's fault or consent, one can recur to a court to obtain redress. By vowing not to defend themselves in civil courts, Ockham seems to argue, the Franciscans have thus wholly given up their rights to property, however much they may continue to make use of its physical benefits. Christ himself, after all, accepted the benefits of this life, though he did not defend them in court.

Ockham's rejection of will rights is quite similar to Luther's, though Ockham's is professedly on a much smaller scale, being confined to Franciscans rather than extended as a duty to all Christians. And, like Luther, Ockham has not eliminated property or justice itself. Under divine law, the Franciscans remain en-

---

25. The source for all these reflections on Ockham and his work is Michel Villey, "Droit Subjectif I," *Archives de philosophie de droit* 9 (1964): 97-127 (reprinted in *Seize essais de philosophie du droit* [Paris: Dalloz, 1969], pp. 140-78). Helpful synopses can be found in Finnis, *Natural Law and Natural Rights;* Golding, "The Concept of Rights"; and Richard Tuck, *Natural Rights Theories* (Cambridge: Cambridge University Press, 1979). Brian Tierney has critiqued Villey's exegesis at length, contesting especially the claim that Ockham was the first to conceptualize rights in a modern way. See "Villey, Ockham, and the Origin of Individual Rights," *The Weightier Matters of the Law: Essays on Law and Religion—A Tribute to Harold J. Berman*, ed. J. Witte, Jr., and F. S. Alexander (Atlanta: Scholars Press, 1988), pp. 1-31. Little in my essay turns on this dispute, however. Tierney's own biases are made clear in his short but helpful essay "Religion and Rights: A Medieval Perspective," *Journal of Law and Religion* 5 (1987): 163-75.

titled to retain their holdings.[26] And even under the civil law, I would imagine that others should in justice leave the Franciscans alone. The only thing that must not take place is for the Franciscans to defend themselves according to human law.

I have added the example of Ockham partially in order to call attention to the profound reflections of Professor Villey that accompany his exposition and that, I think, help us better to understand the situation confronted by Luther as well as by Ockham. Villey connects Ockham's individual power-based notion of a right to his conception of the cosmos as one presided over by a voluntaristic deity—which seems also to be Luther's conception of God.[27] The cosmic and human worlds are made up of individual entities interacting arbitrarily rather than of organizing ideas expressed in human nature and elsewhere, as the ancients thought.

In the ancient view, legal relationships—even those of great personal benefit—essentially involved responsibilities for this order rather than opportunities for the private satisfaction of arbitrary desires. All rights were rights to do what is right, as we might put the matter today. Law was considered a means to (and a part of) the Good rather than a means to the free exercise of will or to the private satisfaction of appetite.[28] What happened,

---

26. Villey suggests, however, that for Ockham this divine law was itself merely a kind of will right of a lawless God, a point contested by Tierney ("Droit Subjectif I," p. 17). Tuck suggests that the earlier Franciscan Dun Scotus still more radically rejected even natural and divine rights to property (*Natural Rights Theories,* pp. 20-24). Yet even Scotus seems to concede natural rules for appropriate use, based on need.

27. See Luther, *The Bondage of the Will,* trans. H. Cole, rev. E. T. Vaughan and H. Atherton (Grand Rapids: Eerdmans, 1931), esp. pp. 230-31.

28. See Villey, "Droit Subjectif I," especially p. 154. Martin Golding has given us a nice example in which we may sense this contrast:

It is plain that the grand ethical systems of Plato and Aristotle do not give the concept of rights any prominence, and the same is true of ancient Greek law. The concept of rights, if present at all, remains below the level of consciousness from the time of the Greek philosophers until late medieval times. For example, in Plato's dialogue, the *Crito,* Socrates is faced with a question that we would put in the following manner: Does a person who believes himself to have been unjustly convicted of a crime have

according to my reading of Villey, is that sometime in the Middle Ages the sense of law as a common project for human excellence was lost, and the idea of *jus* as "that which is right" degenerated into Ockham's (and our) notion of *jus* as a power that is privately possessed.[29] Political society even came to be considered limited by and derived from such individual rights. We can thus appreciate still more deeply Luther's difficult attempts to reconstruct a common project of justice despite emerging concern for modern self-centered rights.[30]

I do not understand Villey to be saying that the ancients were more unselfish than we are today. People then as well as now surely sought personal power and benefits through the law. But the law that they invoked did not elevate this contingent and derivative private advantage to a fundamental principle. In a similar fashion, a legislative lobbyist today often presents arguments based on the common good. Even where self-interest is transparently

---

the right to escape from jail? An examination of Plato's text, however, shows that this dialogue is not formulated in the language of rights. There is no term in the text that literally translates into "a right." Instead, Socrates is concerned with whether it would be right or just for him to escape from jail. Now it might seem, at first blush, that there is only a subtle difference of language between asking whether an act is the right thing to do, on the one hand, and asking whether an individual has the right to do it, on the other. Yet behind this subtlety lies a momentous difference of substance. ("The Concept of Rights: A Historical Sketch," p. 46)

The distance between "must" and "ought" would seem to be less for the ancient view. Cf. note 7 herein.

29. Villey argues that an intermediate step toward this degeneration was the Christian use of *jus* to mean divine commands, or what I have called *duties*. One way to put the point of the earlier discussion of manners would be to say that this allegedly intermediate idea of *jus* can subsist without the *jus* of *either* the ancients *or* the moderns.

30. Underneath the new concern for rights may have been a new understanding of human will and action. No longer believed to seek some good (and properly a rightly ordered good), desire came in Hobbesian fashion to be thought to aim only at itself, only at its own satisfaction. Perhaps this new view underlies Luther's critique of monastic life as well as his hostility to one's personal pursuit of the goods of life. For an analysis of the contradictions inherent in this modern conception of desire, see my essay "A Critique of Fairness," *Valparaiso University Law Review* 16 (1982): 459-81, 464-65.

present, the lobbyist seldom focuses upon his or her private concerns that happen to be advanced by duties to the common good.

From Luther and Ockham I draw a lesson for our purposes. Although there are important analogies between their theories and the one developed in this essay, neither of them attempts entirely to abolish justice itself in order to eliminate the pursuit of rights. Perhaps we ought not be bolder than the Lutherans and the Franciscans. Our somewhat antinomian manners of mutual generosity should not be extended through all aspects of our life together. Arbitrary desiring for oneself should not be replaced only by deference to equally arbitrary desiring by others. Yet even if generosity duties cannot completely replace modern rights consciousness, they may have an important limited use. By their existence here and there in our life together, these courtesies both moderate the litigiousness consequent upon rights and serve to remind us that worlds without rights were once thinkable.

LEGAL DUTIES WITHOUT RIGHTS

I advocate the expansion of generosity duties into the public, legal world. I suggest that we ought to recognize mutual legal duties not to interfere with those who violate certain of their legal duties. It is thus appropriate to look briefly at our present legal practices to see whether such overlapping duties already exist and, if they do, whether they in fact bring about or exhibit the spirit of graciousness we are seeking.

To the best of my knowledge, nowhere in the modern American legal system (by contrast, perhaps, to those of the socialist world or of the Orient)[31] is there a set of mutual duties fully analogous to our cookie or towel examples. Nowhere do duties overlap in a way that eliminates the concept of one correct and nonwasteful legal solution to every conflict of interest. (Liberty rights do not demand waste or a single solution to conflict, but duties are not involved there.)

Nevertheless, there are quite a few partially analogous legal

---

31. Regarding the presence of such duties in the socialist world, Inga Markovits's thoughtful analysis is somewhat discouraging; see "Pursuing One's Rights Under Socialism," *Stanford Law Review* 38 (1986): 689-761.

rules. I made mention early in this analysis of criminal law duties. Many persons have pointed out that these seem to involve benefit rights without will rights, in that individual citizens have no legal power to insist upon enforcement of the penal laws protecting them. But individual self-will is not wholly absent, as it is for tea partiers and for Lutherans, because there is no duty *not* to demand protection or retribution. It is not forbidden to complain to the police; it is only without necessary legal effect. But since a complaint may and does frequently have great practical effect, there is little or no sense that we have no right to protection against the criminal intrusions of others upon our interests.

More closely analogous are those situations in which, although we do no wrong in complaining about others' violations of their legal duties, the state is forbidden or unable to intervene in response. An obvious example is the case of *de minimis* infractions of the law.[32] Here there are no identical duties to leave the same entire buffer zone alone, but there are similar unilateral duties not to enter into what is respectively alien. These duties give rise to no effective remedy where a fence crossing is only slight. There is no point in asking for civil or criminal redress in such situations. No doubt this nonenforcement rule exists largely because any social benefit is not worth the social cost—but also, I think, because of the pettiness, the ignobility of an individual or a system that would make or vindicate such claims. One is reminded of the old maxim "Equity does not stoop to pick up pins." The rule does, therefore, teach and express a kind of minimal generosity in legal relations.

Similarly, one traditional line of case law in the United States recognizes intrafamily tort immunity. A child cannot sue a parent for an injury caused by the parent. The latter is still subject to possible criminal law penalties, however, so the parental duty not to harm subsists—but without a full correlative right on the part of the child. The stated purpose of this immunity is the discouragement of litigiousness and the promotion of family tranquility.[33]

---

32. For example, Model Penal Code §2.12. Note, however, that this code makes punishable even infractions "within a customary license or toleration" if said toleration is "expressly negatived by the person whose interest was infringed," §2.12.(1).

33. The landmark case is *Hewlette v. George*, 68 Miss. 703 (1891).

These last examples may make it seem that I am opposed to the effective enforcement of duties. But there is nothing in the theory here advanced that forbids enforcement per se. Indeed, I think that all duties must sometimes be enforced if they are to be firmly entrenched and if expectations of originally wrongful benefits are not to develop into assertions of rights. It is probably important that last-cookie grabbers sometimes not be invited to the next tea party. But the enforcement of duties to benefit others is tricky, for it may give rise to a rights consciousness (as in the criminal law examples). In other words, nonenforcement of private remedies may be necessary in order to overcome rights consciousness, even though noncompliance with duty may well thus be left without serious penalties. In the best of worlds, there would be some duty enforcement, but never at the behest of the beneficiary of the duty.

There is another class of statutes that impose duties without rights by not providing any *immediate* redress. An Indiana noise control statute is a good example.[34] Although it imposes a duty on all persons not to make "unreasonable noise," no penalty may be imposed until after the allegedly offending party has been warned and has subsequently repeated his or her offense. Initial unreasonable noise is, therefore, a legal wrong against which there is no legally effective protection or remedy. The overall effect of the statute would seem to be to encourage both neighborly toleration of noise and neighborly desistance of noise without any demand for rule enforcement.

Beyond these peripheral matters, there are some important legal duties that do not correspond to anyone's rights. I am thinking here of our duties not to be neglectful, negligent, or reckless. It is common in penal (and more so in tort) law for there to be no penalty for criminal omissions, negligence, or recklessness except in the minority of cases in which these can be shown to have caused harm. Of course, one could argue that our duties here are only to avoid negligently causing harm rather than not to avoid negligence per se. But a duty not to have some physical event beyond one's control occur hardly makes sense. So our duty must be simply to be careful, since this is the only matter under our control, even though we are punished only when harm happens to result from our lack of care.

---

34. Indiana Code 35-45-1-3(2).

When we are merely negligent, when we wrongfully endanger our fellow citizens, they have as yet no legal recourse. Whether we are finally to be punished depends not at all upon their will but only upon the accidental event of possible harm actually occurring. In other words, we all have a duty not to endanger others, but others have no legal will right not to be endangered. And because there exists no way officially to complain about nonharmful negligence, we do not ordinarily imagine that the law has created even benefit rights to have other people be careful. We think, in these areas, primarily about duties, and we put up with a great deal of sloppiness to which we might well object if we thought in terms of rights.

Cigarette smoking provides a good example of a situation in which the law appears to be in transition from the accommodationist style I have advocated to one of precise prohibitions. Smoking, I shall suppose, negligently or recklessly endangers the lives of nearby nonsmokers—that is, I assume that it increases their risk of health problems for no sufficient social purpose. I think there is, therefore, a legal-moral duty not to smoke in public. Yet violation of this duty is only remotely likely ever to be the basis of a private suit or a manslaughter charge, because each smoker's marginal effect is hard to trace. Under such a system, we may well not say or feel that we have a right not to have smokers nearby.

I think this result is appropriate. Although it is wrong to smoke in public, I think it is also ungracious and ungenerous to object to smoking. Though in smoking, smokers perform no useful public function, their private appetites are often so compelling that they ought to be excused by the rest of us—at least as long as we are not involuntarily confined in very close proximity to them for substantial lengths of time.

Many today are not satisfied with this result. They wish instead to see smoking punishable in all cases. I am willing to go along on one condition: that in addition to making smoking punishable we also make discrimination against smokers punishable.

I just suggested that the appetites of smokers ought to be "excused" by the rest of us. The use of that word brings up the last major area of the law in which I have run across duties without rights, and I have found it primarily in European rather than in American law.

An action that is excused (rather than justified) is one that violates a duty but for which punishment is for certain reasons inappropriate—for example, because the actor in some sense could not do otherwise. In our nation, excuse is fairly well confined to duress and to insanity, but in European law it often embraces the broader principle that no one should be punished for not complying with the law where compliance is "too much to demand" by means of the penal law.

One place this doctrine has been applied is that of abortion. The West German Constitutional Court recognized in 1974 that unborn children are included as part of "everyone" in the Basic Law's protection of human life. There is thus a constitutional duty of the state to protect the unborn and a resulting criminal-law duty of women not to have abortions. Yet the same court acknowledged no "subjective right" to life for the child, with the result, as I understand it, that neither an unborn child nor its representative could bring suit to stop an abortion nor to recover damages. Even further, the court concluded that the state need not exact a penalty for abortions committed when the continuation of a pregnancy would have been "too much to demand" ("unzumutbar"). In such a hardship situation, there would seem to be a duty not to kill the fetus without much correlative will right or benefit right not to be killed.

Such a result seems to me quite sophisticated and worthy of serious consideration. The net effect, as intended by the court, is not so much to impose exact limits upon abortion as to *teach* the constitutional legal duty to respect life in every case, whether or not a particular abortion will be punished by law. Insofar as our American "standing" requirements may permit, we should consider retaining constitutional duties while narrowing constitutional rights, so that the law may come to be more a teacher of generosity and less an enforcer of rights.[35]

---

35. For a more complete comparative analysis of the German approach, see my essay "New Constitutional and Penal Theory in Spanish Abortion Law." See also Mary Ann Glendon's very sensitive *Abortion and Divorce in Western Law* (Cambridge: Harvard University Press, 1987). She argues that Europeans in general have considerable political flexibility in the nonpunishment of abortion, perhaps precisely because they do not label it a "right."

Law, Custom, and Mediating Structures: The Family as a Community of Memory

Bruce C. Hafen

This essay explores the relationship between law and the family as a primary community of value in the democratic structure. One might also describe the family as a "community of memory,"[1] not only because we hope family life builds good memories for family members but also because of the part families can play in building—or eroding—the "group memory" of the culture.[2]

I. CUSTOMARY LAW AND FORMAL LAW

It will be helpful first to distinguish between formal law and customary law and to summarize the relationship between those two kinds of law over the past two centuries, with emphasis on the contemporary period. Then we will turn to a description of the family as a mediating structure that plays an interactive role between

---

1. The phrase appears in Robert Bellah et al., *Habits of the Heart: Individualism and Commitment in American Life* (Berkeley and Los Angeles: University of California Press, 1985), p. 282.

2. Alston Chase defines group memory in the case of both a species of animals and a human culture as "the information necessary for survival which is passed on from one generation to another" (*Group Memory: A Guide to College and Student Survival in the 1980's* [Boston: Little, Brown, 1980], p. 10).

formal and customary law. I will attempt to show, among other things, that the declining influence of mediating structures weakens the optimal relationship between law and custom, thereby weakening democracy's ability—like amnesia in the group memory—to sustain meaningful personal liberty over the long run.

A. A Descriptive Model

In discussing the relationship between formal and customary law and illustrating that relationship with reference to certain historical periods, I intend to create a general analytical model more than I intend to treat in detail the history or the philosophical foundations of these concepts. Legal philosopher Lon Fuller has described customary law as the "language" governing human interaction across the entire spectrum of relationships. Customary law is, of course, "not the product of official enactment, but owes its force to the fact that it has found direct expression in the conduct of men toward one another."[3] Indeed, enacted or formal law to a large extent arises from the experience of custom, thus supporting Justice Holmes's observation that the life of the law has not been logic but experience. The legal character of custom originates in both its habitual patterns and its normative quality.[4]

Customary law may be illustrated by long-established patterns of all kinds, from the side of the road on which vehicles drive to the reciprocal expectations that govern our conduct when members of the public stand in line to the business dealings of certain diamond dealers in New York City who work exclusively on the basis of oral agreements enforced only through internal discipline. It is also illustrated in the question directed to a friend of mine by her young daughter: "Mom, do we have to do it because that's just the way things are?"

---

3. Fuller, "Human Interaction and the Law," *The American Journal of Jurisprudence* 14 (1969): 1-2.

4. "There are two sides to the concept of law as interaction," writes Roberto M. Unger; "each corresponds to an aspect of a traditional notion of custom. One element is factual regularity in behavior. The other dimension is normative: the sentiment of obligation and entitlement, or the tendency to identify established forms of conduct with the idea of a right order in society and in the world at large" (*Law in Modern Society* [New York: Free Press, 1976], p. 49).

Formal law, on the other hand, represents all "enacted or authoritatively declared law—what may be called 'made' law"—that is enforceable through the court system.[5] Roberto Unger has further subdivided formal law into (1) "bureaucratic or regulatory law" established by government and (2) the general "legal order or legal system," noting that the distinction between administrative regulation and the broad legal order is a "cornerstone of constitutionalism."[6] My use of the term *formal law* in this essay is general enough to include bureaucratic law along with all the diverse elements of the organized legal system, from contracts and the common law to constitutions and statutes.

A comparison of the natural reach of these two forms of law will illuminate the unique place of the family—and what might broadly be called the laws of the family—within the general framework of law. As the following diagram illustrates, formal law actually governs only a limited spectrum, compared with the complete spectrum of human interaction governed by customary law.[7]

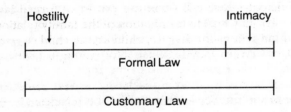

When human interaction reaches the extremes of "hostility" and "intimacy" at opposite ends of the spectrum, it will at some point exceed the natural limits of formal law. For example, international relations are usually conducted in accordance with recognizable formal legal principles, but in times of critical conflict between the command of formal international law and a sovereign government's perception of its national interest, customary law will prevail over formal law. As we learned when Iran ignored the order of the World Court to release the American hostages

---

5. Fuller, "Human Interaction and the Law," p. 1.
6. Unger, *Law in Modern Society,* p. 54.
7. This concept is an extrapolation from Lon Fuller's terminology.

a few years ago, formal international law has only limited power to govern the relationships between sovereign nations. Even at the level of custom, nations almost always avoid the ultimate customary remedy of war, but their resort to the court of international public opinion or their use of economic sanctions and other forms of "alternative [customary] dispute resolution" can be identified and even predicted by students of international custom.

The inability of formal law to govern the realm of intimacy in human interaction is best illustrated by the family, the "organization" and "consciousness" of which is "undermined by the use of legal rules and by the attempt to view relations among persons as relationships of entitlement and duty."[8] If formal law intrudes excessively into family relationships, it can destroy the continuity without which there is no family relationship. However, because customary law, by contrast, "is at home completely across the spectrum of social contexts," it regulates intimate associations in informal ways, including expectations about "roles and functions" that contribute to "stable interactional expectancies."[9] There are, of course, ultimate remedies for the resolution of family disputes that call upon the power of formal law, but such remedies may lead to termination of the family relationship. These include actions for divorce, child abuse, child neglect, and the like. I will return to this theme after laying further groundwork.

Formal law is most at home, then, in the broad middle ground between hostility and intimacy that is inhabited by friendly strangers, whose relationships are best governed by reference to "defined acts, not with dispositions of the will or attitudes of mind."[10] It should further be said of formal law that it draws upon customary law for its nature and existence, which makes an understanding of formal law impossible without reference to its origins in custom. At the same time, a certain level of community disintegration typically occurs as a prerequisite to the rise of formal law, such as "the development of a situation in which one feels increasingly able to question the rightness of accepted practices as well as to violate them. Only then do explicit and formu-

---

8. Unger, *Law in Modern Society*, p. 55.
9. Fuller, "Human Interaction and the Law," p. 33.
10. Fuller, "Human Interaction and the Law," p. 34.

lated rules become possible and necessary."[11] Indeed, the "further one moves away" from extreme normative integration, "the more acute the need for made standards" that are "capable of coercive enforcement by the state."[12]

This observation gives rise to a logical extension: Can formal law stray too far from its origins in custom? Unger has answered that question only indirectly by warning of the dangers to a general system of formal law that arise when law is manipulated by the state:

> If the normative order is construed as a set of tools with which to satisfy the power interests of the rulers, it will lack any claim to allegiance save the terror by which it is imposed. Moreover, it will fail to satisfy the need of rulers and the governed alike to justify the structure of society by relating it to an image of social and cosmic order. The public and positive rules must therefore also be recognized as inherently authoritative, objective, or necessary rather than as made by the ruler according to his conceptions of what is good for himself or for society at large.[13]

For this reason, state regulation has been accompanied in most cultures by "a body of religious precepts. The sacred law is viewed as an expression of the true and right order of things and placed beyond government's reach."[14]

B. Historical Trends

Consider now some illustrations of the relationship between customary law and formal law in American history, because our recent experience may confront us with the problem of excessive separation between formal law and custom. The broad, general pattern of our history reveals a gradual decline in the cultural consensus embodied in our customary law—a decline that has accelerated during the past generation. Formal law, on the other hand, has gradually moved in an opposite direction, increasing its reach and influence especially during the twentieth century.

---

11. Unger, *Law in Modern Society*, p. 61.
12. Unger, *Law in Modern Society*, p. 62.
13. Unger, *Law in Modern Society*, p. 65.
14. Unger, *Law in Modern Society*, p. 65.

These generalizations are of course subject to many important qualifications and exceptions, but they do at least sketch an idea that gives perspective to a discussion of more specific issues.

As a general proposition, the customary consensus during the first hundred years of our national history was more strongly integrated than was our sense of formal law. The widely dominant pattern of rural, agrarian life among a people who shared many fundamental values left only minimal need for regulatory formality. One contrary example may be found in the Constitution itself, which captured in a formal way a concept of national unity that was in 1787 a far more fragile actual assumption than our twentieth-century minds might expect. But to resolve the most divisive issue in our otherwise relatively stable national consensus during the nineteenth century—slavery—the nation finally resorted to the ultimate customary remedy: war.

The outcome of the Civil War led to the adoption of three constitutional amendments, including the Fourteenth Amendment, which established the foundation for major steps along the path of formal law closer to our own day. But for most of the hundred years following the formal acceptance of those amendments, the cultural "customary" consensus about the practical meaning of racial equality lagged painfully behind.

In areas of our national life other than racial discrimination, however, the period from the Civil War until World War II witnessed a significant increase in the role of formal law. Beginning with the antitrust laws in 1890, the laissez-faire economy that had long operated with only minimal regulation was brought within the control of formal law, culminating in the Supreme Court's Depression-driven abandonment in 1937 of the idea that private property (and, hence, private business) was presumptively beyond legislative rule.

As this ascension of formal law in the economic sphere was taking place, the premises behind the nation's customary consensus also changed as the the industrial revolution created a new form of national unity through the emergence of nationwide markets. However, the gradual urbanization and immigration patterns of this era also sowed the seeds of a cultural diversity that would eventually contradict dramatically the appearance of national unity brought on by such formal symbols as close-knit transportation and communication systems.

Developments during the nineteenth century also led to an increasing formalization of American family law, expressed in such areas as marriage formalities and the regulation of divorce, child custody, adoption, abuse, and neglect. These domestic-relations laws contained numerous assumptions about the ideal forms and expectations inherent in family life that have become subject to increasing question in our own day, as we will see shortly. The creation of the nation's first juvenile court in Illinois in 1899 also heralded the introduction of the "child saver" era, in which agencies outside the family assumed formal supervisory responsibility for the welfare of the nation's children.

We have witnessed since World War II a widening gap between the extent of customary national consensus and the extent of formal law in our society. Both trends have been carried by the momentum of earlier directions, although in many ways the pace of change has accelerated, at times with jarring speed. The customary consensus has become increasingly fragmented during a time when formal law has vastly expanded its reach and influence. Despite a modest decline in a few specific forms of federal regulation in the last few years, government regulation since the Depression has become an accepted and pervasive fact of life at every political level and in virtually every sector of public and private activity. In addition, formal law has become the primary medium for private dispute resolution, as "the lawyering of America"—along with a variety of other factors—has introduced us to the litigation explosion and the liability insurance crisis.

The sources of momentum for these developments in the formal law include our welfare state inheritance from the Depression era, the civil rights movement, and the rise of an entire generation of "rights"-oriented groups and individuals who were deprived of social justice at the level of customary law. Developments in our theories of constitutional law during the civil rights era also contributed to the greater use of regulatory vehicles to address private disputes, as expansive readings by both Congress and the courts of the Commerce Clause, late nineteenth-century civil rights statutes, and the state action doctrine all increased the access of private litigants to the mechanisms of regulatory law—which had traditionally been invoked only in relationships between the state and individual citizens. The concepts of class action and public interest lawsuits also brought large new groups into the arena of litigation in cases that frequently gave priority to procedural formalities and symbolic victories, thereby reinforcing the apparent importance of formal law in political and public policy disputes. The idea of such litigation had been powerfully introduced through *Brown v. Board of Education* in 1954, when the Supreme Court brought the full power of formal law to bear in that historic structural intervention into the customary sphere of a segregated society.

But as the influence and visibility of formal law mounted, giving an artificial appearance of unity, our cultural consensus was already beginning in many ways to shatter. The contemporary shattering process represents a sharp focusing of tendencies—direct hits—that were of course moving in our direction many years ago. The entire history of Western civilization since the medieval era represents a general movement toward individual liberation from communitarian forces, a movement carrying elements of both progress and retrogression, depending upon one's point of view.[15] The art, music, literature, and philosophy of the twentieth century represent a questioning and ultimately a fracturing of traditional forms that had been more or less stable for centuries. These abstract expressions have mirrored and anticipated, as art generally does, the movement of traditional assumptions throughout our culture. While that process was long since underway beneath the surface, it has erupted for all to see in our own generation. Robert Bellah and his colleagues plaintively describe it as an "ontological individualism" which has produced a "culture of separation"[16] in which, to use Donne's words, "'tis all in peeces, all cohaerence gone." Or, as Mormon scholar Hugh Nibley put it, the culture was privatized, then polarized, then pulverized.

The cultural fragmentation of modernity is by now well enough known that little documentation here is required. It has both personal and institutional dimensions but has become especially visible in the last twenty-five years as most of the primary

---

15. On this, see Robert A. Nisbet, *The Quest for Community*, 2d ed. (Oxford: Oxford University Press, 1969), especially chap. 4, "History as the Decline of Community."

16. *Habits of the Heart*, p. 277.

institutions of our society have felt its impact. As described by Morton Darrow, the chief forecaster of future trends for Prudential Insurance Company, "Every major institution found itself dealing with people unwilling to blindly accept customary responses." In response, these political, economic, and educational institutions heightened the rhetoric of their public promises only to create an irreconcilable gap between expectations and fulfillment that led to "a lessening of institutional authority which, in turn, caused increased institutional fragmentation under the stresses of the greater complexity of modern, scientific/technological industrial society."[17]

I am particularly interested in the effects of this disintegrating process in the customary law on such mediating structures as religion and the family. I will cite only one illustration in the context of religion and will look more closely at the family. In the Supreme Court's 1985 "moment of silence" school prayer case, *Wallace v. Jaffree,* the majority opinion of Justice Stevens was faced with the task of explaining its rejection of a carefully documented dissent by then-Justice Rehnquist. This dissent had mounted an impressive argument that the founding fathers intended in the Establishment Clause to prohibit the establishment of a state religion and to prohibit a preference of one religion over others, but never intended to require "neutrality on the part of government between religion and irreligion." Justice Stevens made no serious attempt to refute these historical claims, simply stating that, "At one time it was thought that [the First Amendment] merely proscribed the preference of one Christian sect over another, but would not require equal respect for the conscience of the infidel, the atheist, or the adherent of a non-Christian faith." But, he continued, "when the underlying principle has been examined in the crucible of litigation," the Court's prior cases had moved from a concern over "intolerance among Christian sects" to "intolerance among 'religions,'" and finally to a concern with "intolerance of the disbeliever and the uncertain."[18]

This progression of views about the Establishment Clause

---

17. Darrow, "Changing Values: Implications for Major Social Institutions," in *Current Issues in Higher Education, American Association for Higher Education* (1979), p. 13.

18. *Wallace v. Jaffree,* 105 S.Ct. 2479, 2488 (1985).

reflects the ongoing fragmentation of the American consensus about the meaning of religion not only as a legal term of art but as a meaningful concept in our national life. Indeed, the very shrillness of the debate over prayer in the schools could well reflect the frustration many feel in sensing that our cultural evolution is seriously reducing the influence of religion as a cultural force both in individuals' lives and in the customary law. As they perceive an emerging disintegration of the normative consensus, some who yearn to recapture a sense of religious meaning for themselves or for others reach and grasp for some tangible, symbolic, "official" statement that has the normative appearance of— of course—*formal law* in a statute authorizing public prayer. Even those who see the value of religious influence can be genuinely ambivalent about the hopes for such action, because it may be too late for such formalities to matter a great deal, and the focus on formalities may imply that religion is primarily a matter of superficial ritual not much connected to other dimensions of the public experience. On the other hand, a tangible statement, even if only symbolic, may be more needed in times of fragmented consensus than at other times.

C. A Post-Formal Stage?

1. *Family law trends.* We saw earlier that a certain amount of pluralism in the customary consensus is prerequisite to the development of a formal legal system. Since formal law first arose in the American context, our customary law has moved gradually toward further disintegration and our formal law has moved toward heightened influence. The same kinds of forces could well have fueled both movements. At an earlier time in our history, this pattern brought formal and customary law closer together until they were in some theoretically optimal relationship that achieved a productive balance between the personal liberty and the social order that characterize a productive democratic society. Such a relationship might well maintain an appropriately dynamic tension between the "is" of custom and the "ought" of formal law. But as the momentum of both trends has continued in our system, the distance between the two has increased, and constructive interaction between custom and formal law is beginning to falter. As the two sources of law move

further apart, we risk the creation of an unbridgeable gap. What happens then?

Astronomers tell us that a star thrives by maintaining a constant balance between its own gravity, which pulls the star's matter toward the center, and the thermonuclear energy radiating from its inner core, which pushes the matter outward. As long as these opposing forces are in equilibrium, a star remains in full productivity. But when the fusion reactions at the core wind down from lack of nuclear fuel, gravity overpowers the internal radiation, and the star collapses inward. Perhaps custom and law both thrive on some similar optimal, even if at times opposing, interaction.

Recent changes taking place in family law perhaps illustrate what can occur in the "post-formal" stage of a developing legal system, when the distance between formal law and customary law reaches unmanageable proportions. The system appears to experience a mild collapse in the formal law, as we reduce our former aspirations, adjust our expectations, and hope that our newfound realism will lead in a desirable direction.

Carl Schneider has described the "transformation of American family law" since about 1960 through the development of two themes: a "diminution of the law's discourse in moral terms about the relations between family members, and the transfer of many moral decisions from the law to the people the law once regulated."[19] The general shift in American attitudes toward these subjects is reflected in the tone and themes of our movies, TV programming, and popular literature. It can be seen more precisely in the formal law, where our once idealistic attitudes toward divorce, spousal support obligation, and sexual behavior outside marriage have given way to a set of legal norms symbolized by the very term "no-fault divorce," which is now available under one name or another in every state. We are no longer comfortable with Max Rheinstein's observation that our earlier divorce laws were written idealistically enough to keep the conservatives happy but were enforced realistically enough to keep the liberals happy.

These changes have of course reduced the reliance of courts

---

19. Schneider, "Moral Discourse and the Transformation of American Family Law," *Michigan Law Review* 83 (1985): 1803, 1807-8.

and legislatures on moralistic language in family law matters in addition to altering the variables that influence the outcome of legal determinations. For example, child custody decisions involving a cohabiting parent are more likely now to turn on the availability of evidence that the parental conduct would actually harm a given child than on claims that the conduct is immoral. Parental neglect now tends to be determined according to physical and medical evidence rather than evidence of what might once have been called moral neglect. Decisions regarding spousal and child support obligations are more likely now to emphasize short-term needs, thereby implicitly rejecting the assumption of lifelong commitments of mutual responsibility between marriage partners. Concerns about sex discrimination have also altered the once-traditional preference for maternal custody following divorce, even though recent research now shows that this attitude combined with no-fault divorce and reduced expectations about lifelong obligations have in fact resulted in discouraging increases in the economic burdens carried by divorced women.[20]

Family law has generally lowered its confidence in the value of the marriage-based and kinship-oriented model of the formal family. This erosion is partly attributable to an increased sensitivity to the needs of those who once felt the social disapproval of not fitting the ideal patterns. For instance, discrimination against unwed fathers and in the laws relating to children born outside marriage (such as inheritance rights) has been largely eliminated, to the point where the very term "illegitimate" now seems discomfiting. The trend leading to these changes began with a desire to accommodate exceptions to the dominant family pattern but may be approaching the stage where no particular pattern will seem either socially or legally normative.

Many forces have influenced the formal law's recent accommodations in family law. For one thing, the distance between custom and law may have reached something of a post-formal breaking point, altering the aspirational quality of traditional but idealistic legal norms. Max Weber once distinguished between two different levels of moral expectation:

---

20. See Lenore J. Weitzman, *The Divorce Revolution: The Unexpected Social and Economic Consequences for Women and Children in America* (New York: Free Press, 1985).

> All systems of ethics, no matter what their substantive content, can be divided into two main groups. There is the "heroic" ethic, which imposes on men demands of principle to which they are generally *not* able to do justice, except at the high points of their lives, but which serve as sign posts pointing the way for man's endless *striving*. Or there is the "ethic of the mean," which is content to accept man's everyday "nature" as setting a maximum for the demands which can be made.[21]

As we have collectively lost confidence in our ability to practice what we preach, our sense of disappointment has moved us to find another sermon.

The formal law also inevitably reflects significant changes that are the result of long-term trends. The movement from status to contract, for example, has over many centuries shifted the locus of legal identity from an emphasis on social role to an emphasis on individual choice. The family is probably the last vestige of a legal entity based on notions of status, but it now shows the effects of its apparently antiquated origins. A similar trend has shifted our view of marriage from that of a social institution to that of a potential source of individual fulfillment. A recent study of middle-class Americans described as one of its major themes the profound ambivalence most people feel about marriage because of the paradoxical proposition that one can only find oneself by losing oneself. "The more love and marriage are seen as sources of rich psychic satisfactions, . . . the less firmly they are anchored in an objective pattern of roles and social institutions."[22] This individualistic perspective also views the family less as a legal "entity" and more as a voluntarily ordered set of personal relationships. At a more abstract level, individualism challenges the implicit teleological quality of our nineteenth-century family law inheritance, which "until recently . . . relied upon a theory that supposes that the characteristics of the family are given rather than individually or even locally determined."[23]

---

21. Weber, in a letter to Edgar Jaffe in 1907, quoted by Schneider in "Moral Discourse and the Transformation of American Family Law," p. 1819.

22. Bellah et al., *Habits of the Heart*, p. 85.

23. Teitelbaum, "Moral Discourse and Family Law," *Michigan Law Review* 84 (1985): 430, 434.

The emerging acquiescence of formal family law in these deep currents of social change may be necessary to give the law realistic force in helping to resolve the inevitable and increasing disputes that arise in family relationships. When the law in these settings is less personally judgmental and more flexible, the legislative and judicial tasks are clearly more manageable and perhaps more likely to be accepted by those affected by their commands.

Yet there is a poignant quality in the bewilderment one senses in a population reporting that despite their disappointments and their demands, the nostalgic notion of marriage and family based upon loving commitment is, in a perhaps hopelessly dreamy sense, "still the dominant American ideal."[24] Now that the law is perceived not to restrain our almost unwilling self-indulgence, however, its very absence of demands may only compound our sense of hopelessness.

In an earlier time, we instinctively knew the difference between slavery and love, those two forms of bondage at opposite ends of the spectrum of human relationships. For more than a century and a quarter now, we have witnessed effort upon effort to break the real bonds that held some of our brothers and sisters captive to continuing forms of racial discrimination. Having at last set in motion forces strong enough to achieve that essential liberation, it is less clear to us when and how to control similar forces in other contexts. We are now less sure whether the ties of kinship and marriage are valuable ties that bind or ties that lead to sheer bondage. Ours is the age of the waning of belonging.

A stirring and perhaps instructive echo of the phenomenon we have discussed in legal terms appeared in a recent essay by the contemporary poet Stanley Kunitz. Entitling his essay "The Poet's Quest for the Father," Kunitz describes a 1984 anthology of American poetry dealing with the theme of father and son, noting the "revealing statistic" that nine-tenths of the poems were written after 1950. For reasons we can only imagine, "no equivalent selection could have been made in any other period of the history of poetry." Kunitz speculates that perhaps "the filial relationship, being taken for granted in a more stable society, simply did not excite the poetic imagination." But upon further reflection, he finds the modern proliferation of the theme "an authen-

---

24. *Habits of the Heart*, p. 86.

tic cultural manifestation," not as "an occasion for a devotional exercise" so much as "a summons to testify about a failed intimacy, a failed life, perhaps to redeem it through a new effort of understanding."[25]

Kunitz views the father-son poetry as a collective creation of our time:

> With the disintegration of the nuclear family, the symbol of the father as a dominant, or domineering, presence is fading away. Whole sections of our nation are living in fatherless homes as a result of death, illegitimacy, divorce or abandonment. Even when he is physically present in the household, the father may be spiritually absent. . . . Often the father is more than absent; he is lost, as he has been lost to himself for most of his adult life. . . . The son goes in search of the father, to be reconciled in a healing embrace. In that act of love he restores his father's lost pride and manhood. Perhaps he also finds himself.

This is a theme with which Kunitz feels instinctive identification, having himself written as a young man about his own dead father:

>   down sandy road
> Whiter than bone-dust, through the sweet
> Curdle of fields, where the plums
> Dropped with their load of ripeness, one by one.
> Mile after mile I followed, with skimming feet,
> After the secret master of my blood,
> Him, steeped in the odor of ponds, whose indomitable love
> Kept me in chains
> . . . .
>
> At the water's edge, where the smothering ferns lifted
> Their arms, "Father!" I cried, "Return! You know
> The way. I'll wipe the mudstains from your clothes;
> No trace, I promise, will remain. Instruct
> Your son, whirling between two wars,
> In the Gemara of your gentleness,
> For I would be a child to those who mourn
> And brother to the foundlings of the field

---

25. Kunitz, "The Poet's Quest for the Father," *New York Times Book Review*, 22 Feb. 1987, p. 3.

And friend of innocence and all bright eyes.
O teach me how to work and keep me kind."[26]

One hears in these lines an echo of the paradox of loving
bondage, liberating while yet confining: "After the secret master
of my blood . . . whose indomitable love/Kept me in chains"—
and who will "teach me how to work and keep me kind." Perhaps our attitude toward formal law at times symbolizes our feelings about father figures—law that represses in order to teach.
When the father as formal law acquiesces in the resistance of the
child as customary law, perhaps there is the momentary sense of
freedom that, when excessively prolonged, turns toward abandonment. In that sense, the cry for failed intimacy represented
by the new father-son poetry of today may be an anguished reaching out for visible symbols in the post-formal stage, like the quest
for prayer in the public schools.

2. *A stabilizing countertrend.* Before leaving my treatment of
customary law and formal law in their historical relationship, I
need to add at least one important qualification from the family-
law context to the general thesis I have advanced regarding the
movement of these two kinds of law in opposite directions.

Recent developments in family law illustrate the way formal law may reverse its growth trend when it has strayed too far
from its moorings in customary law—or when the customary
consensus has declined to the point of attenuating its relationship with formal law. As we have noted, certain features of family law have thus relaxed their expectations in ways that have become part of—and thereby may accelerate the pace of—the
current cultural fragmentation. In other important ways, however,
family law has shown itself to be surprisingly resistant to these
pressures. For example, despite widespread evidence of a nor-
matively significant sexual revolution, the Supreme Court has
refused to grant the protections of constitutional privacy to sexual
acts between consenting adults. In 1986, for example, the Court
upheld the constitutionality of a state sodomy statute.[27] Moreover,
analysis of the Court's decisions in the areas of parental rights,

---

26. From "Father and Son," by Stanley Kunitz. I wish to thank the
author for his gracious permission to use the poem in this essay.
27. *Bowers v. Hardwick,* 4778 U.S. 186 (1986).

children's rights, contraception, abortion, illegitimacy, and marriage shows that it has based its decisions on interests that grow out of commitments to the importance of marriage and kinship. Even as the cases have come to give protection to decisions regarding the prevention and termination of pregnancy or to parent-child relationships outside marriage, unmarried relationships as such have not been given preferred constitutional status.[28]

In addition, despite some uncertainties about the social meaning of the term *family*, the state laws that define the term in intensely practical ways remain relatively stable. Homosexual marriage is not formally recognized in any state. And the rights of spouses and children under such statutes as inheritance laws, wrongful death laws, and tax laws are confined to relationships based on marriage or biological kinship. Even California's celebrated *Marvin v. Marvin* case was based on a contract theory, expressly refusing to apply the state family law act or to equate cohabitation with marriage. In these and related ways, then, many basic formal law concepts remain as a kind of reinforcing bar that keeps the concrete of customary law more or less together at a time of structural stress.

II. THE FAMILY AND MEDIATING STRUCTURES

I turn now to a discussion of the family as a mediating structure that can play an important interactive role between the realm of formal law and the realm of customary law. The developments we have discussed thus far bear on the kinds of relationships and institutions playing this role as well as affecting the nature of the mediating role itself.

A. Mediating Structures

A few years ago Peter Berger and Richard Neuhaus called attention to the general concept of "mediating structures," those "little platoons," to use Edmund Burke's phrase, that stand between

---

28. See my essay "The Constitutional Status of Marriage, Kinship, and Sexual Privacy: Balancing the Individual and Social Interests," *Michigan Law Review* 81 (1983): 463.

the public and the private spheres. The personal, private sphere is where "meaning, fulfillment, and personal identity are to be realized" for each person. The public sphere, which for Berger and Neuhaus includes the institutions of the national economic marketplace as well as the institutions of government, is made up of megastructures that are "typically alienating . . . [and] not helpful in providing meaning and identity for individuals' existence." Standing between the individual and the megastructures are such mediating structures as families, churches, neighborhoods, and voluntary associations—"the value-generating and value-maintaining agencies in society."[29]

This theme is the modern expression of a central thesis in Alexis de Tocqueville's classic *Democracy in America,* which some contemporary students of middle-class American values regard as "the most comprehensive and penetrating analysis of the relationship between character and society in America that has ever been written."[30] Indeed, Tocqueville is the source of the title for these students' recent study, *Habits of the Heart,* which considers the contemporary status of many issues that interested him.

Tocqueville feared that the strong individualistic strain in democracy could, if unrestrained, tear apart the very connections that hold a free nation together: "Not only does democracy make men forget their ancestors, but it also clouds their view of their descendants and isolates them from their contemporaries. Each man is forever thrown back on himself alone, and there is a danger that he may be shut up in the solitude of his own heart."[31] For Tocqueville, our system's primary source of protection against this risk was the strong interest of the American people in voluntary, intermediate associations, through which "the Americans combat the effects of individualism by free institutions" (p. 509). He found that "Americans . . . are forever forming associations" (p. 513), including not only those that make spontaneous and cooperative

---

29. Berger and Neuhaus, *To Empower People: The Role of Mediating Structures in Public Policy* (Washington: American Enterprise Institute for Public Policy Research, 1977), pp. 2, 6.

30. Bellah et al., *Habits of the Heart,* p. vii.

31. Tocqueville, *Democracy in America,* trans. George Lawrence, ed. J. P. Mayer (Garden City, N.Y.: Doubleday-Anchor, 1969), p. 508. Subsequent references to this volume will be made parenthetically in the text.

approaches to local government or industry but also "the intellectual and moral associations," of which he said that "nothing . . . more deserves attention" (p. 517). Such intellectual and moral associations as those associated with religion and family life were at the center of this attention. The "mores" formed in such places— it is these Tocqueville called "the habits of the heart"—were "one of the great general causes responsible for the maintenance of a democratic republic in the United States" (p. 287), because "there have never been free societies without mores" (p. 590). And family life is central to the development of mores because it restrains the destructive, acquisitive appetites of individualism and develops a sense of personal and civic virtue. Tocqueville maintained that these are the civilizing traditions on which the long-term future of the democratic experiment hinges.

It can still be said in the modern era that the family is "the major institution within the private sphere, and thus for many people the most valuable thing in their lives. Here they make their moral commitments, invest their emotions, [and] plan for the future."[32] The family interposes a significant legal entity between the individual and the state, where it performs its mediating and value-generating function. It remains fundamental to democratic theory that parents, through this institutional role of the family, control the heart of the value-transmission process. As that crucial process is dispersed pluralistically, the power of government is limited. It is characteristic of totalitarian societies, by contrast, to centralize the transmission of values. Our system thus fully expects parents to interact with their children in ways we would not tolerate from the state—namely, through the explicit inculcation of intensely personal convictions about life and its meaning.

B. Mediating Structures, Customary Law, and Formal Law

Let us now explore a few ideas that sketch the place of families as mediating structures, using a model that could also apply— with some variations for different contexts—to other mediating institutions. This model seeks to build upon our earlier look at the relationship between formal law and customary law. We will

---

32. Berger and Neuhaus, *To Empower People,* p. 19.

consider further how the family functions as a community of value in the democratic system, and then I will make a few observations about the declining influence of mediating structures of all kinds in recent years.

The following diagram shows how mediating structures interact with both formal and customary law:

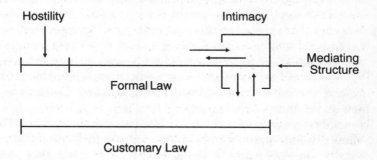

This sketch suggests that the transmission of influence between formal law and customary law that occurs through mediating structures takes place at the intimacy end of the spectrum of human interaction. The mediating structure bridges the line between (in order to mediate between) the formal law and the intimate area of human interaction, although the structure functions primarily within the realm of intimacy. Inside the "box" of the mediating structure, the ongoing family relationships are governed by customary law, but the exterior legal structure is created by formal law. Therefore, the mediating structure engages in two kinds of interaction: (1) interaction with the customary law and (2) interaction with the formal law.

1. *Customary law.* Consider first the two-way interaction between the mediating structure (illustrated by the family) and customary law. Customary law influences family life, because parents, marriage partners, and children all draw on custom in defining their expectations of one another. Obviously those expectations can be altered by explicit understandings, and they allow room for wide individual variations, but parental and marital roles are still influenced heavily by the extent to which the concept of status continues to be felt.

Even the words we use to define familial relationships are

so soaked with implicit expectation that they communicate instantly a level of commitment that characterizes the interactive assumptions fully and uniquely: "He ain't heavy—he's my brother." Or, to take an older example, the dying Christ needed no elaborate explanations, no lawyer to draft a detailed agreement, to communicate his request that his friend and his mother care for one another in a complete and long-term sense: "Woman, behold thy son"; and to his friend, "Behold thy mother." The ancient concept of status told them what to do. "And from that hour that disciple took her unto his own home" (John 19:26-27).

On the other hand, the family reciprocates by influencing the customary law in a pattern that begins with parental teaching and marital interaction inside the mediating structure and then moves through the range of customary experience as family members interact with the larger society in informal ways. The values that both parents and children carry with them in that interaction then seep into the culture with a multiplier effect, like dollars expended in an economy, until those values mold and shape the formal law that grows from its roots in custom. This pattern of extended value transmission shows how mediating institutions influence the formal law indirectly, through what those institutions teach their members.

The doctrine of separation of church and state illustrates this pattern when a church is viewed as a mediating structure. Just as the Free Exercise Clause of the First Amendment asks formal law to stop at the threshold of a church in the name of religious liberty, the Establishment Clause asks that religious organizations influence their members (and society) through the informal means of customary law rather than crossing the threshold back into the formal law in some more direct, structural way. There may be times when a church or a family will interact directly with the formal law, as their mediating role between the public and private spheres suggests, but the more fundamental impact—and most of their mediation—tends to flow indirectly, from the members of the structure down through the customary law and then back upward into the formal law within its appropriate public ranges.

2. *Formal law.* Having noted the general pattern of interaction between customary law and mediating structures, consider now the basic relationship between the formal law and mediat-

ing structures. This is, not surprisingly, primarily a formal relationship, because the formal law authorizes, creates, and protects mediating institutions—and then, for the most part, leaves them alone. That our system of formal law should recognize and sustain their institutional freedom is a constitutional principle of crucial significance.

Under our theory of government, the state is not the primary source of the substantive values that give meaning to individual lives. Indeed, the state is discouraged by such doctrines as the separation of church and state from establishing official value positions. The totalitarian state, by contrast, gladly and aggressively assumes the role of imposing on all its citizens "one comprehensive order of meaning."[33] The guarantees of the Bill of Rights are primarily process-oriented values—liberty, equality, due process, free speech, and the like—that define the terms on which the state must deal with its citizens. At the same time, however, these protections consciously seek to assure each individual citizen of the governmental protection as well as the freedom necessary for his or her own pursuit of personal meaning and fulfillment. These procedural and structure-establishing values are an essential means toward the end of personal self-determination.

Yet the influence of the democratic state has today become so pervasive, and our customary value sources so fragmented, that the process-oriented values of the Constitution that "inform and limit" the governmental structure are thought by some scholars to be the "values that determine the quality of our social existence."[34] As a result we live in something of a value vacuum. The "megastructures" of society (which may include corporate conglomerates and large labor unions as well as large governmental bureaucracies) have overpowering influence—yet they do not typically seek to tell us what our lives really mean. Corporate activity is primarily economic, despite its obvious social consequences, and is more concerned with means than with ends in the pursuit of personal meaning. Perhaps it is no wonder that modern society feels so much personal loneliness and aliena-

---

33. Berger and Neuhaus, *To Empower People*, p. 3.
34. Fiss, "Foreword: The Forms of Justice—The Supreme Court 1978 Term," *Harvard Law Review* 93 (1979): 1.

tion in light of the fact that these vast, meaning-neutral agencies have grown to proportions of boundless influence at the very time when other large-scale forces have introduced widespread feelings of uncertainty and fear about the meaning and the long-term security of both individuals and the culture.

Still, our constitutional theory does not leave individuals totally to their own resources in the personal quest for purpose. The right freely to pursue personal meaning is embodied primarily in the values of the First Amendment (augmented by the Fourteenth), which are usually regarded as a set of individual liberties, and yet our constitutional tradition also recognizes and protects the intermediate structures—those "intellectual and moral associations" of which Tocqueville wrote—which, through their own institutional traditions and group cohesiveness, have been the primary "value-generating and value-maintaining agencies in society."[35] These meaning-oriented constitutional values protect not only individual religious liberty but the institutional liberty of churches, not only personal academic freedom but the institutional liberty of schools and colleges, not only individual freedom of speech but the associational freedom of groups and the institutional freedom of newspapers, not only the personal right to seek meaning and education but the institution of marriage and the institutional right of the formal family to direct the moral, intellectual, and spiritual development of its children. The "little platoons" are a deliberate part of the structure, for they nurture the values that ultimately sustain the entire system—as well as sustaining the personal quest of each citizen. For these reasons, the theory of our formal law protects these institutions from excessive governmental regulation as well as from other forms of harmful intrusion.

In addition, of course, our constitutional theory has reflected a careful balancing of individual and social interests in establishing the standards that determine the kinds of institutions and relationships that are entitled to such extraordinary protection. The test used for making such determination is very significant because of the way it defines the relationship between customary law, formal law, and mediating institutions (of which more shortly).

---

35. Berger and Neuhaus, *To Empower People*, p. 6.

In general terms, there are only two categories of exceptions that will cause the formal law to pierce the veil of protection that guards the private enclaves inhabited by mediating institutions: serious harm to the individual members of their groups or serious conflicts with overriding governmental policies. Thus, the interest of parents in freely rearing their children is subject to such limitations as are necessary to prevent child abuse and enforce compulsory education laws. The interests of churches and educational institutions are subject to various forms of government regulation, especially when the regulations pose no material threat to the religious or educational mission of the institution. As a group's purpose moves further from the First Amendment's special interest in political, religious, and intellectual freedom, its protections are correspondingly reduced. For example, the "commercial speech" of business corporations is a less-protected form of speech. The freedom of association within a marriage or a political group has greater protection than associational freedoms between unmarried couples or among members of a civic club.

Constitutional theory requires a state to show that it has unusually compelling reasons for intervening in these protected relationships. There is a similar reluctance to allow formal legal enforcement of personal claims against the mediating institution arising from its alleged harms to its own members. For example, relationships involving familial intimacy are not supervised by the state unless serious abuse is inflicted or the relationship itself is threatened. The reasons for this reluctance relate to the overriding commitment of constitutional theory to the value of encouraging continuity within the protected sphere, because that continuity is essential for mediating institutions to perform their functions.

Consider, for example, the marriage relationship. Much of what family members—especially married partners—"owe" one another cannot be enforced in a court of law. Yet a traditional sense of family duty has throughout history demonstrated a remarkable power to produce obedience to the unenforceable. The commitments of marriage and kinship have taught parents and children values learned only through truly "belonging" to a larger order. The very nature of these values requires that they develop voluntarily. For such reasons, the formal law stops at the family threshold not merely because it *should not* regulate intimate relations but because it *cannot* regulate them without impairing their very existence.

The courts have ordinarily recognized these limits on the reach of formal law, even though the cases make it clear that we sometimes pay a high price for the concept of family autonomy. For example, an Alabama court refused to resolve a difference of opinion between two parents about whether their child should attend a private school or a public school, invoking the traditional rule that judicial intervention is inappropriate until there has been "a failure of that natural power and obligation which is the province of parenthood. . . . The judicial mind . . . is repelled by the thought of disruption of the sacred marital relationship."[36] And in *McGuire v. McGuire,* a favorite case among teachers of family law, a Nebraska court refused to order an elderly husband to increase the level of financial support he gave his wife, so long as they still lived together, because "the living standards of a family are a matter of concern to the household, and not for the courts to determine." He refused, among other things, to take her to the movies or to buy an indoor toilet, sink, or electric refrigerator.[37]

Is the Nebraska court sustaining the family autonomy essential to a mediating institution, or is it sustaining Mr. McGuire? Tocqueville would probably argue for the former interpretation. He believed that Americans "think that in the little society composed of man and wife, just as in the great society of politics, the aim of democracy is to regulate and legitimatize necessary powers and not to destroy all power" (p. 601). He believed that this pattern—despite its obvious impositions—belonged to a larger purpose that is more difficult for our egalitarian minds to perceive than it might have been in 1840:

> The Americans do not think that man and woman have the duty or the right to do the same things, but they show an equal regard for the part played by both and think of them as beings of equal worth, though their fates are different. . . . While they have allowed the social inferiority of woman to continue, they have done everything to raise her morally

---

36. *Kilgrow v. Kilgrow,* 268 Ala. 475, 107 So.2d 885 (1959).
37. *McGuire v. McGuire,* 157 Neb. 226, 59 N.W.2d 336 (1953).

and intellectually to the level of man. In this I think they have wonderfully understood the true conception of democratic progress.

For my part, I have no hesitation in saying that although the American woman never leaves her domestic sphere and is in some respects very dependent within it, nowhere does she enjoy a higher station. And now that I come near the end of this book in which I have recorded so many considerable achievements of the Americans, if anyone asks me what I think the chief cause of the extraordinary prosperity and growing power of this nation, I should answer that it is due to the superiority of their women. (P. 603)

The marriage cases illustrate the basic theory of institutional autonomy among mediating structures, even though the cases from Alabama and Nebraska are somewhat dated and even though the general availability of divorce today makes it highly unlikely that a marriage partner will be kept unwillingly in legal bondage. The ready availability of divorce does suggest, of course, a substantially scaled-back commitment in the formal law to the institutional preservation of marriage as a social institution. Intervention in child-parent relationships, on the other hand, has become less predictable as a result of conflicting legal currents. Heightened public interest in protecting vulnerable members of society has increased the interest in the enforcement of child abuse laws, but a corresponding increased interest in protecting personal privacy against bureaucratic intervention has raised the standards a state must satisfy to justify intervention.

In general, the institutional authority of mediating structures has gradually come to receive less support from the formal law. No small part of the formal law's growth in recent years has come at the expense of paternalistic authority wherever it has been found, from public schools and juvenile courts to churches and families.[38] A discussion of the law's recently developed but deeply felt suspicions about paternalism is beyond the scope of this essay, but we should at least note the risk that

---

38. See my essay "Exploring Test Cases in Child Advocacy: A Review of Mnookin, *In the Interest of Children,*" *Harvard Law Review* 100 (1986): 435.

at some point the law's unwillingness to sustain discretionary, paternalistic authority in private institutions impairs the capacity of those institutions to fulfill their purposes. Our society has, with good reason, now given such priority to the prevention of abuse of discretionary authority, public or private, that it is hardly fashionable to raise such a question. But the question needs asking in a discussion of mediating institutions. Our collective inability to answer it thoughtfully is one of the reasons the potentially positive influences of mediating structures have been reduced.

C. The Purposes of Mediating Structures

Perhaps one reason the recent erosion in the strength of mediating structures has met with less resistance than Tocqueville might have expected is that the nature, purpose, and positive value of these structures were taken so much for granted that as their influence began to wane, we hardly knew what was happening to them, much less why we should defend them. Elements at the bedrock of our social tradition in this way are less visible to the eye than the clouds of individualism that have blown across our intellectual landscape.

Our consideration of the interplay of mediating structures with the customary law and the formal law as distinct forms of interaction has at least introduced a general idea of the institutions' purposes, both for the benefit of the individuals involved and for the benefit of society. The more specific purposes served by each kind of mediating institution—family, church, school, voluntary association, and the like—deserves to be explored within the context of the particular institution. The scope of this essay allows for little consideration of institutions other than the family, but some further, though abbreviated, reference to the mediating purposes served by formal families might be appropriate.

I have elsewhere sketched some of the connections between marriage, kinship, and the purposes of a democratic society.[39] These connections emphasize what Roscoe Pound

---

39. See "The Constitutional Status of Marriage, Kinship, and Sexual Privacy."

once called the "social interest" in domestic relations, as distinguished from the "individual interest," which is much more obvious to the modern mind. Consider in an illustrative way three elements that suggest why we have thought of the "formal family" as a legal entity—an organized institution in the "mediating structure" sense, rather than a loose collection of individuals having no commitments to one another except those enforceable by formal law.

First, children need the structure and assumptions of permanence produced by the institutional quality of the formal family. A child's need for continuity and stability in the parent-child relationship is widely documented in legal and nonlegal literature. It is a need so great that disruptions of the child-parent relationship by the state, even when there is inadequate parental care, frequently do more harm than good. The needs of children are seldom treated in contemporary policy debates regarding informal adult relationships, but this factor is so essential to the collective "best interests" of our children that it alone may justify the incentives and preferences traditionally given to permanent kinship units based on marriage.

Second, as alluded to earlier, family life is the source of public virtue—a willingness to obey the unenforceable. The individual tradition is at the heart of our culture, yet the fulfillment of individualism's promise of personal liberty depends upon the maintenance of a corollary tradition that requires what may seem to be the opposite of personal liberty: a willing submission to duty and a sense of obligation to interests larger than one's own. The family is a key source for maintaining the tradition of duty, because it is in family life that parents, children, and kinfolk taste through sometimes bittersweet experience the sweet fruit of commitments that transcend personal interest. As Michael Novak has described it, "My bonds to [my wife and children] hold me back . . . from many sorts of opportunities. And yet these . . . bonds . . . are . . . my liberation. They force me to be a different sort of human being, in a way in which I want and need to be forced." Novak also sees in this personal development "the political significance of the family," because "a people whose marriages and families are weak can have no solid institutions." Family life is "the seedbed of economic skills, money habits, attitudes toward work, and the arts of financial

independence," and parent-child roles are "the absolutely critical center of social force."[40]

The forceful momentum of individualism, however, has in
recent years privatized attitudes about family life in ways that un-
dermine the tradition of duty. While legal attitudes toward marriage once "turned on the importance of marriage to society,"
more recent cases "turn on the importance of the relationship to
the individual."[41] Robert Bellah and his colleagues found that
married Americans are increasingly adopting the "therapeutic
attitude" that the essence of love lies in the "sharing of feeling
between similar, authentic, expressive selves—selves who to feel
complete do not need others and do not rely on others to define
their own standards or desires." Those who have adopted this
view tend to equate self-sacrifice with neurotic self-effacement
and reject it as a barrier to genuinely healthy relationships. "In
its pure form, the therapeutic attitude denies all forms of obligation and commitment in relationships, replacing them only with
the ideal of full, open, honest communication among self-actual-
ized individuals."[42] Clearly this attitude erodes the capacity of
marriage and family life to develop general attitudes of other-
directed commitment, and Bellah and company conclude that
"What would probably perplex and disturb Tocqueville most
today is the fact that the family is no longer an integral part of a
larger moral ecology tying the individual to community, church,
and nation."[43] At best, today's atomistic attitudes see the family
as a "haven in a heartless world."[44] To serve as a genuinely integral part of the moral ecology, the family structure should be
a bridge between the individual and the community rather than
a one-way street that draws privacy into the family enclave but
gives little in exchange.

Third, formal marriage and kinship-based family life create
politically and legally significant entities between the state and
the individual. Because the democratic system has allocated the

40. Novak, "The Family out of Favor," *Harper's*, April 1976, p. 37.
41. "Developments in the Law—the Constitution and the Family," *Harvard Law Review* 93 (1980): 1156, 1248-49.
42. *Habits of the Heart*, pp. 100-101.
43. *Habits of the Heart*, pp. 111-12.
44. The phrase is that of Christopher Lasch; see his *Haven in a
Heartless World: The Family Besieged* (New York: Basic Books, 1977).

responsibility for children's early socialization to the family rather than to governmental agencies, the power of the state to shape the attitudes of its citizens is significantly limited. Today this limitation is more real in theory than it is in practice, because the pop cultures that characterize the mass media and the public high school are shaping a remarkably monolithic value orientation—such as it is—among the nation's young people. This kind of national uniformity is hardly the result of conscious political theory; it more probably reflects the value vacuum that results from the reduced influence of traditional mediating structures combined with the recent withdrawal of child-oriented agencies (including the schools) from attitudes and practices involving affirmative value transmission. It is also aggravated by the declining influence of parents in the socializing role.

Even so, in terms of our political theory and our legal structures, the place of the formal family is potentially powerful. As D. H. Lawrence put it,

> The marriage bond . . . is the fundamental connecting link in . . . society. Break it, and you will have to go back to the overwhelming dominance of the State. . . . Perhaps the greatest contribution to the social life of man made by Christianity is—marriage as we know it. . . . [This] little autonomy of the family within the greater rule of the State . . . has given man the best of his freedom, given him his little kingdom of his own within the big kingdom of the State.[45]

Legal concepts such as marriage and minority status also act as sources of objective jurisprudence, protecting intimate relationships from being treated as if they were business dealings that are constantly subject to litigation. The relatively permanent commitments involved in marriage allow both society and the legal system to make important assumptions about the relationship, including the assumption that it should be left alone. If the law could not discriminate among points along the spectrum of "intimate associations," our biological and psychological ties would become unceasingly tangled and subjected to judicial supervision, as if the entire population were a series of split families all involved in one

---

45. Lawrence, *Apropos of Lady Chatterley's Lover* (1930; reprint, Brooklyn: Haskell House, 1973), pp. 35-36.

continuous hearing on support, custody, and visitation privileges. The more our relationships of intimacy are seen by the law as relationships among "friendly strangers," the more legalistic—and less intimate—the relationships will become.

Minority status is a family-related concept that also allows objective standards that reinforce the notion of "role" among children and parents. In the absence of age-based standards, children would be engaged in even more frustrating battles than the ones they feel they are now in, with state agents, parents, and children all vying for power in ways that would make normal psychological development impossible.

D. The Declining Influence of Mediating Structures

The increased emphasis on formal law has been fueled by an increased emphasis on individual rights, which looks with suspicion upon the institutional character of mediating institutions. The regulatory element of the formal law has also developed increasingly intrusive attitudes toward private organizations, in large measure motivated by understandable concerns about abuses of discretionary (customary) power. Thus, the major historical developments that have added force to the formal law have at each step reduced the scope of previously unregulated activity. The post–Civil War amendments to the Constitution reduced the power of state governments, post-Depression constitutional theory reduced the power of private business, and the civil rights era reduced the scope of institutional discretion in a number of ways.

These forces eroded the influence of mediating structures from the (formal) megastructure side. Their influence was simultaneously eroding on the (customary) private side through the fragmentation of shared values and the emergence of distrustful attitudes toward institutions in general. As the megastructure of government grew through accretions to the formal law, fears of government's institutional power were in some ways transferred into fears of all institutional power.

For example, Laurence Tribe foresees a coming liberation by the state of "the child—and the adult—from the shackles of such intermediate groups as family." Tribe's commitment to individual autonomy as the supreme constitutional value moves him to advocate for each person a right of liberation "from domination by those closest to them" in the entity of the formal family, even though he also acknowledges the need for legal recognition of "alternative relationships" that "meet the human need for closeness, trust, and love" in the midst of "cultural disintegration and social transformation."[46] In this vision, the formal family is suspect for the same reasons that the governmental megastructure is suspect: all institutions, public or private, are seen as the common enemy of individual rights.

This tendency to lump all institutions together in a pejorative way not only obscures the general distinction between the public and private sector but more specifically obscures the distinction between mediating structures, which should augment the development of self-identity and personal meaning, and megastructures, which should protect individual self-determination by maintaining a free environment. This obscurity has two adverse effects on the influence of mediating structures. For reasons discussed earlier, it impairs the processes, relationships, and associations necessary to the long-term development of personal value systems. It also impairs the democratic process itself: "Without institutionally reliable processes of mediation, the political order becomes detached from the values and realities of individual life. Deprived of its moral foundation, the political order is 'delegitimated.' When that happens, the political order must be secured by coercion rather than by consent. And when that happens, democracy disappears."[47]

The role of schools as mediating structures is directly related to the role of family life, but schools have lost mediating influence for particular as well as general anti-institutional reasons. As part of their fundamental childrearing role, parents have long enjoyed the constitutional right to direct the education of their children. Largely for this reason, the schools to which parents sent their children were traditionally regarded as serving *in loco parentis*. In this sense, both private and public schools originally assumed in a functional sense a mediating-structure role as extensions of the family.

---

46. Tribe, *American Constitutional Law*, 2d ed., University Textbook Series (Mineola, N.Y.: Foundation Press, 1987), pp. 974-80, 987-90.
47. Berger and Neuhaus, *To Empower People*, p. 3.

In more recent years, in part because the schools have been called upon to assume a primary role as direct state agents in the desegregation of American society, the structural place of the public school system has become less clear. We are uncertain today whether a public school is an extension of individual families and therefore part of the value-oriented private sphere or whether it is an extension of the state, which makes it part of the more value-neutral megastructure. Clearly the public schools today are by law and in practice primarily extensions of the governmental mega-structure. However, many parents and others still assume that schools should play a value-transmission role more typical of a mediating structure. The reality is that public schools are now cast in both roles, with some segments of the public expecting them to be value neutral while other segments expect them to take strong value-oriented positions. Such structural ambiguity has become the source of tension and ambivalence in the minds of teachers and administrators as well as in the public's perception.

Another example from the context of religion is also instruc-tive. Mark Tushnet has explained that the dominant influence of Protestantism throughout American history has given our view of the First Amendment's religion clauses a distinctly individ-ualistic flavor, since Protestant theology typically emphasizes a direct connection between the individual and God. In the Catho-lic, Mormon, and Jewish traditions, by contrast, a greater role is played by institutional or communal forces.

This anti-institutional tendency is reinforced, in Tushnet's view, by the assumption of the liberal tradition that a free market economy is most likely to flourish when personal economic de-cisions are made according to self-interest and without inter-ference from such intermediate institutions as churches. The republican tradition, on the other hand, would allow more shap-ing of individual lives by larger orders, which creates more un-derstanding of institutional religion. The ascendency of the liberal tradition over the republican tradition in our history has therefore led to confusion about the meaning of religion as a category of constitutional interpretation.[48] It has also contributed

---

48. This point is established by Mark Tushnet in a paper delivered to the Section on Law and Religion, Association of American Law Schools Annual Meeting, New Orleans, 5 Jan. 1986.

toward the reduced influence of churches as mediating institutions.

E. Sustaining and Threatening Long-Term Individual Liberty

1. *The family and social continuity.* In attempting to strengthen the role of mediating structures, we should give priority to those institutions (other than the overtly political institutions of the megastructure and the formal law) that are most likely to sustain individual liberty in the long run. The family and religion seem especially well suited to this role, because they are most likely to encourage the aspirational morality and the group memory necessary for social survival.

Indeed, most religions teach that there is something unusually sacred about the duties we owe to those who stand in kinship with us. The Old Testament tells us, for example, that God commanded ancient Israel to "honour thy father and thy mother: that thy days may be long upon the land which the Lord thy God giveth thee" (Exod. 20:12). Malachi also prophesied that Elijah would "turn the heart of the fathers to the children, and the heart of the children to their fathers, lest [Jehovah] come and smite the earth with a curse" (Mal. 4:6).

It would repay our efforts to explore more than we have the relationship between the enduring liberty of society and our attitudes toward both our progenitors and our posterity. The preamble to the Constitution states that the nation's charter was adopted to "secure the Blessings of Liberty" not only "to ourselves" but also to "our Posterity." We think differently about the nurturing of liberty when we think of ensuring freedom for our posterity rather than only for ourselves.

The ancient Greeks also believed that reverence for parents was all bound up with, and perhaps symbolized, reverence toward other universal forces, including natural law and divine power. The story of Oedipus the King, for instance, teaches much about the relationship between reverence for parents and reverence for the gods. The curse brought upon the city of Thebes by the acts of Oedipus against his parents (or against the prophetic power of the gods) is not unrelated to the idea of the earth being cursed when the hearts of the children are not turned toward their fathers. Those who respect their parents are likely to respect other natural, universal influences. In the latter part of the Oedipus story, the blind old king goes willingly at the hand of his faithful daughter, Antigone, to the place appointed by the gods for his death. This time his submission to the gods, paralleled by the loving support of Antigone for her father, leads not to a curse but to a miraculous blessing on the land where Oedipus is buried.

Such aspirational values in family life nurture the larger social vision of commitment to the good of the larger order. Religious values ultimately have similar purposes. Because of the contribution these values make toward lengthening the days of a society and ensuring the blessings of liberty for posterity, they are of a different quality from values oriented only toward individual rights that lack clear linkage with social interests. With this in mind, the Supreme Court has limited the protections of due process liberty as a substantive right to interests arising from marriage and kinship,[49] while rejecting that same protection for sex outside marriage.[50] Similarly, the Court has refused to extend the protections of the First Amendment to obscene speech—not because obscenity is not literally "speech" but because obscenity has not "the slightest redeeming *social* importance."[51]

In its family privacy cases, the Supreme Court has relied on a test oriented toward tradition and the purposes of a democratic society in defining which claims are entitled to the extraordinary preference of being within the meaning of due process "liberty."[52] Such treatment can be viewed as placing the family privacy cases within a constitutionally protected mediating structure; in any event, it serves to put such claims presumptively beyond the reach of all but the most compelling state regulatory interests. This form of constitutional liberty is located outside the explicit text of the Constitution, but its origins are in the customary law—for these rights are part of a "pattern so deep-

---

49. See "The Constitutional Status of Marriage, Kinship, and Sexual Privacy."

50. As in *Bowers v. Hardwick,* 478 U.S. 186 (1986).

51. *Roth v. United States,* 354 U.S. 476, 484 (1957); italics mine.

52. See "The Constitutional Status of Marriage, Kinship, and Sexual Privacy," pp. 463, 545-60.

ly pressed into the substance of our social life that any Constitutional doctrine in this area must build upon that basis."[53] The established standard recognizes only those fundamental liberties that are "implicit in the concept of ordered liberty," such that "neither liberty nor justice would exist if [they] were sacrificed."[54]

2. *The case of homosexuality.* Among the most significant contemporary threats to a sound ordering of the relationship between customary law and formal law is the Supreme Court's occasional willingness to expand constitutional protection in individual rights cases that lack strong connections either to the customary law or to values and social structures that encourage the development of long-range personal liberty. The most dramatic illustration of this kind is *Roe v. Wade,* even though the right to an abortion can also be viewed as arising from kinship-related interests in protecting decisions about childbearing.[55]

The most recent similar instance was the 1986 case of *Bowers v. Hardwick,* in which the Court upheld by a 5-4 margin the constitutionality of a state sodomy statute. The intense reaction against *Bowers* among many advocates of individual rights and the closeness of the justices' vote suggest that the sexual freedom issue may be presented to the Court again before long. Among the most deeply felt arguments opposing the *Bowers* decision is the claim that the majority's reliance on a tradition-oriented test for determining constitutional privacy runs directly counter to the central meaning of civil liberties in the contemporary world, because such a test is inherently majoritarian.[56] This position, whether applied to homosexual relations or to casual sex outside marriage, takes fundamental issue with the very idea that social interests rooted in the customary law should influence the formal law in regulations of personal behavior. It also rejects the idea that mediating institutions should be given preferred constitutional status in order to build upon and nurture values drawn

---

53. *Poe v. Ullman,* 367 U.S. 497, 546 (1961) (Harlan, J., dissenting).

54. *Palko v. Connecticut,* 302 U.S. 319, 325, 326 (1937), quoted in *Bowers v. Hardwick,* 478 U.S. 186 (1986).

55. See "The Constitutional Status of Marriage, Kinship, and Sexual Privacy," pp. 527-37.

56. This point was made in a paper delivered by David A. J. Richards, Section on Gay and Lesbian Legal Issues, Association of American Law Schools Annual Meeting, Los Angeles, 6 Jan. 1987.

from aspirational morality in the customary law. Moreover, it reorders our thinking about a system of family law still largely based on kinship and marriage, because it accepts as an equal a pattern that rejects both biological kinship and intimate relations based on long-range commitments.

For such reasons, the homosexual sodomy case—or the same argument in any consensual adult sex case—represents the logical extension of the individualistic currents that have challenged both the customary consensus and the traditional framework for determining the boundaries between the formal law and the area of intimacy. If this argument is accepted, it will have captured the force of formal law by virtue of its post-formal stage, where it has drifted too far from customary law to be bound by those connections. It will also accelerate the disintegration of the social consensus by altering deeply held customary norms regarding one of the oldest of moral issues.

When such arguments were presented earlier in our legal history, they were taken far less seriously, perhaps because customary law and formal law stood in a closer relationship to one another. That they could be taken so seriously today accurately reflects the uprooted state of contemporary laws and customs.

The Story of an Encounter

Edwin A. Rodriguez

In the spring of 1987, twenty-six scholars and practitioners of the law gathered together for a two-day conference in New York City exploring, among other things, the possibility that the law itself has become morally "lawless."

Pastor Richard John Neuhaus opened the conference by emphasizing its theme, "law and the ordering of our life together," and by encouraging the participants to advance the state of public debate on this issue.

A SOCIOLOGICAL SLANT

After Neuhaus's introductory remarks, Susan Silbey of Wellesley College reviewed her essay. At the conclusion of her review, Neuhaus suggested two questions that might guide the ensuing discussion: (1) "Do we agree with Silbey's depiction, on purely empirical grounds, of how the law, formally conceived, has an out-of-syncness or at least tension with 'living law,' and is that our situation today—that these two are out of sync in some way serious enough to create or to warrant the term *crisis*?"; and (2) "If so, why is that the case, and what does it mean in a society such as ours in which, presumably, legitimacy—governmental legitimacy, including legal legitimacy—is derived from the consent of the governed, who might have different notions of what constitutes the law?"

119

Richard Stith of Valparaiso University School of Law kicked off the discussion by addressing Silbey's treatment of the sociology of law and its connection with legal realism and modernity. "I am thinking back to Peter Berger's *Rumor of Angels,* in which he talks about the relative and the relativists, and I wonder if, in trying to understand what the law is and where it is going, it isn't very important to reflect on the sociological, ideological, and other factors that make sociologists look at the law the way they do. Are those the same factors that operate in causing legal realism to become dominant in law schools? Sociology and legal realism seem to have purposely rejected the notion that we ought to analyze facts, empirical data, in conscious reflective equilibrium with our perceptions of objective value." Tying sociology and legal realism to modernity, Stith then asked, "Why has modernity tried to construct the thought system that we know as social science? Is that something worth exploring?"

Silbey responded that the motives underlying modernity certainly are worth exploring, and she proceeded to elaborate on the connection between legal realism and the sociological view of law as well as social science in general. "As to the specific question of the sources of this instrumental vision of law and its connections to legal realism, they are intimate. While the roots of the sociological, empirical, and instrumental end up being closely connected with the origins of social science, I am not sure it could have succeeded as an intellectual enterprise without the support of legal realism at the turn of the century. Recently I've been drawing a very close connection between the legal realists and the contemporary empirical scholars and I've been rereading works in the two different strands that one can find in legal realism—the jurisprudential strand of reading the text as formal law and the strand with a technocratic vision of society. It seems to me that contemporary, empirical studies of law have picked up on the strand of the legal realists, the technocratic strand, and have left silent the jurisprudential reading."

Enter Historicism

Martin Golding of Duke University Law School joined the discussion by suggesting another element in the development of the sociological view of law in the United States. "What Oliver Wendell Holmes was doing in his early work on the common law was very much influenced by the kind of historical thinking that was dominant in academic circles in a variety of fields in the nineteenth century, particularly in the late nineteenth century. This view held that if you looked at law from a historical perspective and saw its development, you couldn't possibly maintain the commonly held views about law. Those who wanted to look at law in terms of its historical development got a more varied, chaotic picture. Accidents of history played a great role, and one couldn't think of the law either as a mirror of freely given values or as necessarily having inherent values; it was something much more complex. Was there some truth in Phil Selsnick's remark that the sociology of law has some special affinity with the natural-law tradition?"

At this point, Neuhaus interjected, "Before anyone tries to answer that question, there are two things that we might want to discuss: relativism and the relativizing of the relativists, to use Peter Berger's happy phrase. Martin Golding is suggesting that that began with historicism, that historicism is the foundation of the relativizing impulse. That in itself, I think, is an important proposition. Is that the source of it with regard to contemporary law?"

Silbey answered by saying that while she agreed with Selsnick's view that the sociology of law is closely connected to the natural-law tradition, she disagreed with his overall understanding of the sociology of law. "I think he mischaracterizes a large part of the sociology of law. He takes a very generous and benign view. I consider it a much more political project."

Harold Berman of Emory University Law School addressed the issue of historicism that Neuhaus had introduced, tying it in with Justice Holmes. "The courts look back to the past and carry on a tradition. Legal philosophers tend to say this is to be explained by the will to power or by reason and justice, and not in historical terms as a historical phenomenon itself. I think it is appropriate to mention just that point while thinking about Holmes, because in a way Holmes was essentially a positivist who believed that morality is dictated by the authorities, by the state, and that law is essentially the will of the lawmaker corresponding to the social mores prevalent at the time. He used historical material because he had to explain American and English law, which have a very strong historical element. It seems to me that Holmes was demystifying history, showing that all historical concepts developed in time for reasons wholly different from what was supposed and that looking at the real history behind their development gave them very different connotations from what was commonly supposed. In a way, he did away with history by this kind of relativist explanation of the historical dimension of law. In that sense I think it is possible to think of Holmes as a realist, but I think that the word *historicist* is a good one if you think of historicism as the use of history without any subservience to history. The historical school of legal philosophy, on the other hand, was developed in Europe under the influence of Burke in England, and it assumed that history has direction and meaning."

"And it need not be morally relativized," said Neuhaus.

"Right, history dictates that we do this," said Berman. "I think that it is essentially something like a providential view of history—that history has certain lessons for us. It sends us in a certain direction, it moves us at a given time."

Joining in concerning Holmes, Golding stated, "One thing that is important and perhaps connects Holmes with the more technocratic view of law is that he believed that once we see how things develop historically we can free ourselves from the past. If we see how arbitrary and accidental all this was, then we should be more free to do what we want."

"So you can use the past in order to undo the past," said Neuhaus, "or at least to undo its normative hold on you."

At this juncture Edward Gaffney of Loyola Law School brought up the concept of law in the biblical tradition. "This tradition describes law more or less along the lines of Silbey's third model, a sociological approach. Law is not ascribed to the king in Israel but rather to the source of love that binds the community together. Law throughout the ancient Near East was classically the work of the monarch enacting decrees. In Israel, however, it was the task of the prophet, primarily the prophet Moses, to whom are ascribed all of the divergent historical developments of law within ancient Israel. This is reflected in the tradition that exegetes have identified as the Elohist code, a collection of case law. Certainly law functions in this context as the glue of the society, bonding people together in covenanted life. The norms of the covenanted community may be quite clear and precise in what is called apodictic law, or thou-shalt-never sorts of commands. However, even there law is not eternal, immutable, and absolute within the Greek concept. Rather, it reflects divergent approaches. The rich interpretation of Torah by the prophets and the rabbis should give anyone pause who is inclined to think that we are within reach of some comprehensive view of how to order society in one quick fix."

Neuhaus built on Gaffney's comments. "Your point is that the three sources of legitimacy or the three ways of thinking about law and morality are not adequate, as Professor Silbey spells out. This biblical way is another way."

"I'm not suggesting that what she's saying is inadequate," Gaffney responded. "I'm saying that the tradition which often colors American social judgments about law, which is primarily used to legitimate what we think about norms in our society, is in fact not treated in her essay. The biblical tradition does not present us with a monolithic bunch of clear norms. It reflects historical developments over time and preserves a considerable pluralism within its very growth and development. And yet this is the tradition to which the evangelical right makes explicit reference when it addresses the breakdown of Enlightenment models.

"Professor Silbey suggests that law is a political project. That is absolutely correct with respect to the biblical tradition. For example, the eighth-century Assyrian crisis provoked the need for having more clearly in mind what the norms of the northern tribes were going to be, and we get them in clear form precisely with the obliteration of that whole group of people. It is precisely when the Assyrians are on the wane that we get the Deuteronomic reform and a major new political activity establishing a covenanted community that is not predicated on going along with the culture but rather on the distinctive character of faithfulness to religious norms."

The Moral-Political Project

Mr. Robert Bork, formerly of the District of Columbia Circuit of the U.S. Court of Appeals and now at the American Enterprise Institute, picked up on the theme of law as a political project, asking Silbey, "In what sense is it enlightening or new or insightful to say that law is a political enterprise? In one sense, I don't see how law can ever lose its moral legitimacy. All law comes out of an idea of what morality requires, even the most technical regulations. I suppose you can say law loses its moral legitimacy in the sense that it may be used by a particular interest group for self-interested reasons which conflict with others, but law always has some morality. It may not be a majority's morality; it may be a special-interest morality.

"I would like to understand in what sense exactly we're worried about the separation between law and morality. I agree with the thought that we had known for a long time that law was a political and moral enterprise, and I am not quite sure in what sense that is new."

Silbey replied that she meant something very simple. "I meant it in the sense of studying the way in which law has been studied—not law itself but the way in which professionals have constructed the discourse about what they do. For example, Mr. Bork's comment that the law has always been moral is not something that would be universally agreed with. To make a universal claim like that could in fact be construed as, itself, a political project."

"I suppose anything can," said Bork.

"That's right," replied Silbey. "So just naming it is insufficient. The task is to identify all the elements behind it."

Commenting on the Bork-Silbey exchange, Neuhaus noted that it raises "a very basic question about what it is that we're doing here. Is it assumed in the various worlds of pertinent discourse that law is a moral-political enterprise?"

In addressing Neuhaus's question, Berman added a third element to the legal enterprise. "It has been argued by some that law is only a political enterprise. It's been argued by others that law is only a moral enterprise, that if it is not moral in some sense, it is not law. I would like to argue that it's both of those, and it's also a historical enterprise. I would argue that there are political, moral, and historical ways of interpreting law. It may be that there is no such thing as law, that there are only politics, morality, and history. This is one of the problems with Ehrlich's living-law conception, which Ms. Silbey accepts. Ehrlich said, Let's not only look at statutes and cases; let's look at the way that people actually behave with respect to each other. In that sense one might say that he dissolved law into this whole relationship. In any case, to say that law is politics doesn't help us out. The important question here is whether law is more than politics, more than morality."

At this juncture, Dr. Charles Emmerich of the Center for Church/State Studies at DePaul University Law School commented on the relationship between law and morality. "I think that law and morality are inextricably connected. Whether law recognizes it or not, it is carrying out values. What is perhaps most fearful is when law carries out values without knowing why it is doing it or what the values are. Whether or not law has a consciousness of doing it, it is doing it."

Following up on Emmerich's statement, Gaffney sounded a note of caution. "One of the problems that strikes me is the intriguing notion that we are value-neutral or free of value in the communication of that which is supremely valuable, that which arises out of the historical confrontation between politics, morality, and law. I want to emphasize the point that many of my colleagues on the law school faculty side of that enterprise perceive themselves as detached, dispassionate, disinterested transmitters of that which has inner meaning free of value. That is itself part of the difficulty of the ungluing of the moral force of law. That is what our students pick up on—this subtle, maybe even overt, notion of what law is—and they take from the law only that which is valuable for them: getting ahead fast in a fast-moving society, maximizing profit, and the like."

Following Gaffney's remarks, Neuhaus stated that "Law remains a discrete tradition. There is an identifiable, continuing discourse about it which is institutionalized. It is an enterprise. I think this is an important and very provocative line of argumentation, and it ties in very closely with our understanding of law, society, and community. You have a number of identifiable, discrete traditions with names on them, such as education, religion, and law. If there is a problem we're addressing, it is that the institutional sphere and the tradition called law are not in living conversation with other institutional spheres and traditions that constitute the community."

Responding to Neuhaus's comment, Stephen Arons of the University of Massachusetts at Amherst referred to the relationship between law and morality. "It was mentioned that there is a necessary connection between law and morality, so in dealing with your question, it might be useful to explore whether that connection between law and morality is, in a worldly context, constructive or destructive. There is an old Chinese saying that when the way is lost, then comes the law. We may very well be dealing with a connection between the collapse of community and the rise of a kind of bureaucratic, positive law."

"Your Chinese saying put me in mind of the word *halakah*," said Neuhaus, "which is usually translated 'law' but really means 'the way to go,' the way to be and the way to go. There is some sense in which people in our society think the law should have that kind of halakic character, that law is a kind of normative way to go and not simply a technical institution that intervenes when people have lost their way. To the extent that people don't see the 'way-to-go-ness' inherent in the legal process in a democracy, you have problems."

Continuing the discussion about the relationship between law and morality, Lynn Buzzard of Campbell University School of Law said, "One thing I think we have to distinguish is whether we mean that law has ceased to converse in moral terms or that law in fact no longer has any sort of moral character to it or that law is no longer legitimized by morality. I am not sure that we are separating these questions, which I think are clearly different. Second, I am instinctively inclined by my own tradition and beliefs to think that law is in serious trouble, as related to moral foundations. Yet, in some respects I see a society, in both lawmaking and Supreme Court decisions, in which moral factors are given more articulation than they might have been one hundred years ago. The people I might be inclined to be nervous about—the judicial activists, who are not the old law-as-an-omnipresence-in-the-sky people—are the people who in the civil rights movement, in labor law, in environmentalism, and in so many areas appear to reflect a broader world of reality at times, including moral elements, than justices did one hundred years ago, even if they aren't using as much explicitly moral language as I might like them to. I find it difficult, sometimes, to jibe that with my sense of nervousness about them. Maybe part of that nervousness stems from the fact that I'm not sure where they're getting these moral elements—or where they're going to get them tomorrow. Maybe I need to be more nervous about where they'll find them tomorrow than where they find them today. Today they're drawing on a moral tradition that is part of our Western heritage, but if that pool is being depleted, where will they find the moral elements tomorrow?"

Following Buzzard's remarks, Bork pointed out a negative consequence of tying law and morality too closely together. "The introduction of moral argumentation into the courts is simply a device to free judges from law to legislate as they wish. That is all it turns out to be, and I think it is utterly inconsistent with the judge's function. It means that he has just cut himself loose and is on his way. That may be why the people who use that form of argumentation make me nervous."

"Well, I understand that," said Buzzard. "It also creates a tension for me, because I want law to have been developed with a consciousness of the moral imperative. But I am not inherently uncomfortable with the judiciary recognizing that moral imperative."

"But they should take the moral imperative from the law that they are given," Bork responded. "Insofar as a judge engages in moral reasoning, he should be engaging in moral reasoning to see whether this situation is like the moral principle that has been placed in his keeping. When he begins to ask what the law should be—what constitutional law should be, for example, in the light of our tradition—he begins to make himself over into a very activist or imperialistic judge who will not be reflecting our legal tradition. He'll be reflecting, in fact, what Irving Kristol calls the 'new class morality.'"

"I understand those arguments," Buzzard countered, "but in certain contexts—the Nuremberg trial, for example—another part of me can celebrate a judge saying, 'I don't care what the little law said, it was not the *law*.' There is something in me that responds positively to that."

Aristotelianism and America

Neuhaus continued the session by posing anew a central theme of the conference. "Let me suggest that maybe what we're talking about is our common assumption that law is a political-moral enterprise. It is part of politics in the Aristotelian sense of rational agents engaged in deliberation over how we ought to order our lives together. Obviously, the very title of the conference has that kind of Aristotelian tone to it, pointing to the fact that we are engaged as a community, as a society, in rationally deliberating over how we ought to order our life together. Law is part of that process of deliberation, an identifiable, discrete part of the process. Maybe the question is something like this: Is the law today, specifically in America, contributing constructively to the communal deliberation over how we ought to order our life together, or is it not? If not, why not; and what might be done about it?"

Golding took up the question, enlarging its scope somewhat. "I'd like to address the question by broadening it a little bit and by raising another one. I think we can identify different forms of dispute settlement. Let me suggest a range going from adjudication in the courts, the kind of zero-sum adjudication with a winner and loser, to labor-management relations, and all the way to family therapy. In each of these different forms of dispute resolution the aim may be different on the part of the dispute settler. The ways issues get formulated are different. We have different forms of community reflected in these different methods or modes of dispute settlement. In certain of these, rights language or claims language may be appropriate. In others it won't be. When we talk about community on a large scale and ask whether law impedes or does not impede, I think that we have to ask what kind of community we are talking about. Is it the community of strangers or is it the community of intimates? Another consideration is that we are always members of a variety of different communities. What I am suggesting is that there are different kinds of community, and that law may have an appropriate place in one form and not in another."

Arons engaged Golding's comments. "I feel uncomfortable with the conclusion that Professor Golding seems to be reaching with the multiplicity of communities that we might be referring to when we talk about the separation between law and morality. There's a kind of underlying tension about the absence of a moral discourse about the things that are most important in our society. When anybody says that there are multiple communities and therefore it may be impossible to have this discourse, it always seems to me a fatalistic, almost nihilistic kind of conclusion to reach. Nevertheless, I think Professor Golding's point is right, and I would like to extend it another step by making a historical observation.

"There is something peculiar about the present status of American society, peculiar even from the point of view of one hundred years ago. Our society is so radically fragmented, not just in the ways previously suggested, but specialized in so many different ways, that we don't really have a shared community of values. It is in that sense, now, that it becomes extremely difficult to participate constructively at all in a moral discourse. I think that in the absence of an underlying consensus about the most basic kinds of values—that is, the axiomatic values as opposed to the values that we can talk about rationally as second-nature assumptions—the law has nothing to deal with. So it becomes an enterprise of imposition. That's a rather melancholic conclusion to reach, but I think that historically it's probably accurate. If you read some discussions about developments since the late nineteenth century in the American studies field, I think you find evidence to support the argument that there is no 'American Mind,' there is no common set of values that we can adhere to. That tends to leave us very troubled about our inability to talk about these things, except in very narrow areas."

Neuhaus challenged Aron's comments. "It's frequently said by the courts, as well as by many others, that we have this new situation of radical moral pluralism—not simply religious pluralism, but moral pluralism. And yet social science research indicates that this is not the case at all. There's a remarkable consensus concerning elementary morality in the United States. The question is whether the social description is not itself a powerful factor in law inasmuch as it has been legally declared to be the fact in the face of empirical evidence to the contrary."

"I happen to think that there is a national consensus, at least insofar as the First Amendment and other parts of the Bill of Rights are concerned," said Emmerich. "That the society will respect freedom of speech and assembly and will accord religious freedom are basic value statements."

Bork reentered the discussion by commenting on the constraints on moral discourse at the community level. "One of the difficulties is that, to the extent that the court moves out and produces constitutional law beyond that which original intention would suggest, it nationalizes morality and takes away the ability to have moral discourse from communities that do have shared values. The moral discourse then occurs at the Supreme Court, or within a group I might call the 'constitutional enterprise' or apparatus, which is a small group of judges, lawyers, academics, and journalists. The moral discourse of this group presents a very different view of morality than is found in many of these small communities. In that sense, it is not a moral discourse; in fact, the law is *discouraging* moral discourse in the community where it would otherwise occur. Now, whether it's a matter of talking at the national level about issues that differ regionally and locally or a matter of the knowledge class having a different center for its morality than others, I think you can see again and again, particularly in the Religion Clause opinions, a drive toward moral optimism or the fraternization of morality. You see the same thing in First Amendment speech cases and in the nonestablishment and free-exercise cases. This is not moral discourse. It's the denial of the utility of moral discourse."

Picking up on the issue of federal infringement on state and local responsibilities, Stith commented, "I don't think that there's a way we can reinterpret the First Amendment to be communitarian, because the federal government was never meant to build community. It was a kind of a treaty among communities that was very restricted in the values it was supposed to impose. Then by some bizarre historical circumstance, through the Fourteenth Amendment, we find that the values of this federal contract are somehow supposed to limit what state and local actions are supposed to be, which is crazy. We've got to develop in constitutional law the notion that there's a much stronger restriction on what Congress and the federal executives can do. Otherwise we are imposing a big, distant, federal, contractarian set of values, which was never meant to form community. We are setting up sledgehammer restrictions on any possibility that a lower level institution might do more. The point I am trying to make is that the Constitution should be viewed primarily as a restriction on the federal government. I am not suggesting that the states should then be the primary focus of community, because there might be other mediating institutions which the federal courts should leave alone as well. When we start to talk about what constitutional law is going to do, we're going to have to talk, in some sense, about political communities. You can't talk about law without thinking in some sense about political community."

Neuhaus restated Stith's point: "There are significant communities—even legally recognized communities—that are not part of the formal polity; and law, especially at the national level, ought to have as its first axiom to do no harm and give as much leeway as possible to these mediating structures."

Mary Ann Glendon of Harvard Law School concluded the first session of the conference by adding a cross-cultural dimension to the discussion. "It strikes me that the difficulties we're having in identifying tradition or society or community are specifically American kinds of difficulties, at least difficulties that have a particular kind of poignancy in the American context. As a legal comparatist whose subjects include Western Europe, what strikes me about our discussion and the subject matter is the special kind of American dilemma we're encountering—that as a people who have few things to bind us together, we tend to look to law as a value carrier in our society much more than most other people in their societies. But the same things that make us look to law as a value carrier make it hard for law to operate that way. When we try to search for the common values that are embodied in law, we tend to come up with such things as neutrality toward diversity or an emphasis on individual rights. This exaggerated emphasis on individual rights, the community of strangers, is just another way—an inside-out way—of looking at it. It has an attitude about diversity that we all like, but it may prove to be threatening to the kinds of communities and mediating structures that Professor Hafen has written about."

THE TEMPTATIONS OF CANAAN

After Neuhaus's introductory remarks, Tom Shaffer, then of the School of Law at Washington and Lee University and now at Notre Dame Law School, summarized his essay. At the conclusion of his presentation, Neuhaus suggested to the participants that they might want to engage a subtheme arising from Shaffer's paper: "There is an interesting issue that's very much related to community, communities, and normative discourses within communities that constitute traditions. In the whole debate over religion and law in America today, there is in the right-of-center religious community, the so-called Religious Right, a strong group, very influential, although small in numbers. (I'm not aware of anyone in this room that might be counted among its representatives, at least not in any outspoken sense.) They usually call themselves theonomists and very seriously believe that liberal democracy is a heresy, a fundamental departure from Christian truth. They maintain that the nation's law should be reconstituted on the basis of what they call 'Bible law.' In some ways, Tom Shaffer's argument is sort of a theonomy of the left—namely, that on the one hand there is the law for the particular people, which has priority, and on the other hand there is the law in the civil realm, which is akin to the law in Canaan inasmuch as it is suspect at best and potentially idolatrous. It's an interesting kind of position, and it should be entertained because it's part of the new insurgency of religion in American public life, which I take to be an empirically demonstrable fact beyond a reasonable doubt. From both the left and the right as the political spectrum is ordinarily defined, there is this theonomic, theocratic, Bible-law view. It stands over against an understanding of the church in which Christians try to live as alien citizens of two realms. In that understanding we talk about two kingdoms, or natural law, or general revelation, or all the other ways we have of dealing with that. That bundle of questions is very much caught up and I think very usefully posed to us by Professor Shaffer's paper. He ends up, naturally, logically, with a rather pessimistic view of the question posed earlier—namely, whether law can contribute to deliberation over how a community ought to order its life together. The answer Tom gives us is 'Perhaps, but probably not very much.' The 'particular people' should be concerned with keeping its own house in order, and Canaan will take care of its business. We have to think about that very carefully, because we are still dealing with the issue of traditions making public claims of truth having to do with the ordering of communities."

Tradition and Law

Berman started the discussion by pointing out what he felt to be an inadequate treatment of tradition in Shaffer's essay. "While our conception of tradition starts at the same point, Professor Shaffer stops his theological memory, as far as I can see, with the

New Testament. Of course I understand that he was not offering a systematic presentation of the history of the church. But his references to everything after the New Testament era were given in very negative terms, starting with regret concerning the baptism of Constantine, dismissal of the Roman Catholic church-state relationship in the Middle Ages as pagan, and the charge that Congregationalism, or at least the Reformation, sold out to local government. I wonder what happens to tradition at that point. It seems to me that there's a very great danger of going back to some ancient tradition and denying the continuity of that tradition. I see tradition, including our own constitutional tradition in the United States, as being in some sense evolutionary. The idea is that tradition has to be adapted to the new circumstances that continually arise.

"I also have difficulty with his treatment of the conflict between law and religion. In some very basic sense, the law is idolatry, the law is Canaan, and religion is grace. But what about the law of the people of Israel? The Jewish and Christian traditions both ascribe the source of law to God himself and speak of divine law. Indeed, I think one of the great threats to the legal tradition in America today is that in the past sixty years—and no further back than that, I think—Americans have stopped thinking about law as derived from some larger tradition such as the Ten Commandments, the Bible in some sense, English common law, or some other sort of mysterious development of the past that is handed down to us. Rather we've come to think more and more of laws as having been made up by people at a particular time, maybe in the past or maybe today, maybe by legislators or maybe by judges. If you ask most Americans today where our law comes from, they would likely name Congress or the courts or something of that kind. Sixty or seventy years ago, in my childhood, people would have said it came from the Bible.

"Well, then, where does our American law come from— the Bible, Roman law, English common law? In both the Judaic and Christian traditions the law has (or is supposed to have) its source in some cosmic, universal order. That's the tradition of law. It seems to me that Professor Shaffer has gone over to a kind of radical Reformation bordering on Mennonite thought, convinced that the law is somehow of this world, the earthly kingdom, and it's depraved and fallen, and the particular people are the people who are preserving their prophetic and witnessing role in the face of that situation. Incidentally, this seems to me to have no relationship to the Jewish people, who make no distinction between secular and sacred in that sense. The welfare of the people and the spiritual life of the people are supposed to be combined, and there is no technical separation, it seems to me, in that tradition. Such separation leads to the conclusion that in a liberal democracy, law cannot provide community in theory or in practice.

"I'm very discouraged by the thought that the law cannot provide community and should not attempt to. I think this neglects a very important aspect of law and the source of law. While the law alone cannot provide or somehow guarantee community, it can conserve community. The law can help to make community possible, can provide the context in which community becomes possible. This is the basic Judaic and Christian conception of law, and I don't think you really need to make a distinction between the moral law, the Mosaic law, and the human law that is traditionally developed and enacted in the light of that higher law. Law and morality together provide a context in which it's possible for people to live in justice and peace and love. This is the hope for the law. If we abandon this view, we take too narrow a view of law, we take law out of the tradition. Western legal tradition, which I think is endangered in the twentieth century, has understood the law to be closely related to the prophetic witness that Professor Shaffer is advocating."

Neuhaus thanked Berman for his comments and added, "I think there is something we may want to come back to in Professor Berman's first point, about whether the approach recommended by Professor Shaffer isn't itself a betrayal of the memory that he asserts is so critical to the particular people. Another thing that deserves more consideration is Berman's suggestion that the common attribution of the source of the law has shifted from the Bible to Congress and the courts during the past sixty years. I think it's interesting that if you ask the American people where *morality* comes from, well over eighty-five percent of them will say the Ten Commandments, the Bible, the teaching of the church, or something of that sort. That very graphically illustrates the divorce of law and morality that has taken place during that sixty-year period."

Singing in Exile

At this juncture, Gaffney took issue with Berman's criticism of Shaffer's paper by pointing to the diversity and subtlety of the biblical concept of law that his essay brought to light. "Okay, Harold Berman has a problem with Tom Shaffer's paper because he feels that it stops too short, that it stops at the formation of Canaan with the Bible. My first problem came a little bit earlier still, with the fact that he stopped on the verge of Canaan, before we even got into the development of the biblical Canaan.

"The reading of the biblical text shows that there was considerable divergence in the development of the law in ancient Israel, and one of the things that we have to learn, that might be entirely relevant to Professor Shaffer's argument, is that when the people of Israel entered Canaan, they were wary to be sure, but they went on to appropriate the customary law of the ancient Near East to a great extent. I'm not saying that they duplicated it precisely; to the contrary, they reflected it with the kind of subtle tension that Professor Shaffer talks about, and that's what I think is really the genius of his essay. He is not talking, I think, about a repudiation of living in the community. He's talking about being careful, being wary, being mindful, being truthful and faithful about who we are in the transmission of memory, lest we be swallowed up by the practices of the Canaanites. The Deuteronomist would condemn a particular king even if the king had engaged in terrific building projects and constructed schools; what it really boiled down to was whether he was encouraging the practices of the cult of prostitution and the like.

"In our time, we are less like the people on the verge of entering Canaan than we are like the people in exile. We don't live in Jerusalem, we don't have a temple to go to to sustain our faith. We live with the Babylonians. We live, therefore, with the double injunction of the prophets of that period, Jeremiah and Ezekiel: first, we are to remember who we are, that we are a part of this people; and second, we are to care about the city, which is also a prophetic injunction to the people who find themselves estranged from Jerusalem. Exiles resent the fact that their captors ask them to sing the songs of Zion. They're incapable of doing it; they choke up at that very idea. 'Sing about Zion?' the exiles say. 'You're the ones that have enslaved us and brought us over

here. We don't want to be here. But while we're here, we're not
going to become Babylonians.' That, of course, is the genius of
biblical law."

James Burtchaell of the University of Notre Dame also commented on Shaffer's views. "I think that the essay could be en-
hanced by some reference to the season in which it was written,
because we're experiencing changes in the very issue that you
raise. The Christian churches—especially those with a more historically conscious intellectual tradition, who know that they are
churches of development—are presently emerging from a phase
in which they've tended toward patriotic admiration of the
American way of life. It's interesting that at the same time the
scientific method is being challenged. Some years ago one of my
colleagues, a mathematician, informed me that Notre Dame has
one of the best collections of mathematics periodicals in America.
'There are 103 of them that you have to have,' he told me. 'I mean
there are only 103, and we have 100 of them, from volume one,
number one.' As chairman of the library committee, I swelled
with pride when I was told this. But then he told me that all the
volumes go to the warehouse after three years because nothing
older than three years in mathematics is worth reading, except
for the historians. Such obsolescence frightened me, because in
my discipline I don't want to read anything that young. And I
think that sentiment is spreading. I think that the readiness to
believe the latest is giving way to a concern for a wisdom tradition. More people are willing to believe that memory gives us access to better thinking than was once the case. And in keeping
with this, Christians are now much more ready to criticize
American tradition and insight, and that's a very novel turn for
many American communities."

"And you see this represented in Professor Shaffer's
paper?" asked Neuhaus.

"No, I'm improving the paper by making its author more
conscious of that," Burtchaell replied with a smile. "Professor
Shaffer speaks of particularity, but in a sense he understates it.
He refers to *a* particular people, but we all know that there are
many particular people, and some of them are quite particular
about being distinct from one another. Nor are these particular
peoples all nationals; indeed, most of them are not, and some
pointedly wish not to be understood nationally—international

labor unions and parties and the like, many of which are considered suspect and subversive because of that.

"Judaism and Christianity in this case are of special historic interest. Judaism was an *ethnos* that resisted all assimilation. Christianity did it somewhat differently. Within its very first generation it followed the Hellenistic synagogue pattern in the local communities. But as soon as the Gentiles and Jews consented to dining together once a week in the name of Jesus, they took the drastic new step of being gathered out of every tribe and nation and not being thoroughly at home in any of them—not because they were an *ethnos,* but because they refused to be an *ethnos.* So our two particular peoples are very special in the course of the development Shaffer tried to describe.

"Lastly, Shaffer overstates the particularity, a point I think several people have already expressed some concern about. The particular people that Tom has most in mind are Christians and especially Catholics. That particular people follows a conviction and stands on a commitment which it commends to its neighbors and its fellow citizens as a standard they would be wisest and happiest to live by. Their Christian community champions some insights that others do not share and maintains that these are not merely insights into the ways Christians have chosen to live but rather that they are insights into the way we all need to live. If they are wrong, they are wrong on those grounds as well as on others. Christians understand themselves as a community favored with particular disclosure of how all human beings ought best live in society as well as in the community. In that sense, I think, particularity is not the only appropriate description of the community that Professor Shaffer has learned most from."

A Place for Liberal Democracy?

Next in line, Walter Berns of the American Enterprise Institute addressed a question to Shaffer. "Beginning as you do within the religious tradition, and thinking about this question from that point of view, would you arrive at a liberal democracy such as the United States of America?"

"You mean if I could write the history of the polity of the particular people?" Shaffer asked.

"Well, I mean a little more than that," said Berns. "For example, you say at the outset of your essay that the principal mandate of the law is to preserve, in memory and teaching, a ritual calendar and a narrative sequence of events. It seems to me that sort of thing is much more readily done in a political organization other than the United States of America. So I'm asking about the compatibility of what you're talking about with what I would like to think we are here in America. Beginning from where you do, would your thought culminate with liberal democracy?"

"Probably not," said Shaffer. "In principle it wouldn't, because liberal democracy's anthropology is that the human person is radically alone, is radically his own king, and the particular people have always seen themselves as radically connected, radically together."

"Well, that disturbs me," said Berns, "because this liberal democracy was described by Abraham Lincoln as the last best hope of earth. And I think that's accurate."

"Well, Lincoln's a clinical example there," Shaffer responded, "because I think Lincoln's view of the American people was very biblical."

"But it's not compatible with the view that you're advocating," Berns suggested.

"I think the religious tradition does not regard liberal democracy as the last best hope of man," said Shaffer. "The last best hope of mankind is the coming of the Messiah."

Berns then raised his central question. "What has to be done by each member of a particular particularity in order to live with all the others? Do we—your particular group, my particular group—not have to give up something in order to live together in peace? I didn't find that point addressed in your essay."

"I would say that particular people are willing to help with community," Shaffer answered. "What the particular people are not willing to do is bow down to idols. And what the particular people may well not be willing to do, as this history develops in modern America, is kill."

The debate continued for a while with Shaffer arguing in favor of the unlimited right to civil disobedience by particular peoples and Berns arguing for limits to civil disobedience in order to preserve liberal democracy.

Reflecting on the exchange between the two, Buzzard stated that "A Christian theology of the Cross certainly invites a separationist, almost isolationist view. I think that has to be balanced with a Christian notion of creation, which invites a kind of engagement and a refusal to separate the spiritual from the material, the political from the religious. I am concerned that Professor Shaffer's essay doesn't reflect a sort of theology of the state. I think one of the problems we have is the lack of a theology of the state, frankly, and particularly in the more conservative evangelical parts of America which grew up on the frontier, without much interest in the city of politics, almost with an anti-urban, antipolitical mood.

"My evangelical tradition was very strong on prayer meetings and gospel songs and speculation about when Jesus was coming back. We turned over to other people things like government and schools and science and the arts. It seems to me that some sort of an unholy deal was cut somewhere. The government said to the church, Well you can have piety and prayer and gospel songs, but you'll have to stay in your place. As long as you stay in your place we'll get along fine; but, there'll be trouble if you stick your fingers into education or science or government. And the evangelical community bought that and said, Hey that's a wonderful deal. But it turned out not to be a wonderful deal. Today I think the evangelical community is trying, even if it's stumbling a lot and occasionally making an ass of itself, to develop a public theology."

Neuhaus asked Buzzard, "Why did it turn out not to be a wonderful deal? Why couldn't they have just kept on doing that?"

"It was a lousy deal theologically because it forgot lordship, creation, community, society, and culture," replied Buzzard. "Moreover, it was a lousy deal not simply for the church but for society as a whole, because it cut out of public discourse precisely the kind of prophetic and moral conversation that I think is critical for culture and society. Both the church and the state were losers."

America, the Community?

At this point Golding spoke up: "I'd like to reflect a little bit on Tom's description of communities of faith as certain key events memorialized in liturgies, teachings, celebrations of worship, and so forth. There is, I think, more than simply some kind of community metaphor at work here; it's more like an analogy between the notion of a special, peculiar people with its memories of certain key events and what we have experienced as American people in terms of our own history. The American people are not simply religious; America is religion itself. Cryptically, what we have is the final dispensation or secularization of salvation history in this particular experiment called America. Perhaps the sorts of phrases that have already been cited, such as 'the new Israel,' 'mankind's last best hope,' and 'Yahweh's chosen people,' are not to be taken merely as rhetoric but as descriptive of what the American people truly believe.

"I would like to suggest that the key liturgical events we celebrate—such as the Civil War, America's crucifixion by religious analogy, if you will—may create for us a nation, a people apart from our natural communities, a sense of belonging, the only real basis for sharing anything together. What we have in America is essentially a kind of secularized religion, in a way that's different from what has developed anywhere else in the world. Of course the question, coming back to Professor Shaffer, is how we proceed if this is true. All the earlier critics, like Bellah, who have talked about American civil religion have characterized it as a kind of secular religion in a pejorative way, in a critical way, as idolatrous. But I wonder: If we didn't have something like these secular myths that are analogues to biblical and Christian understanding, would we have America at all? Would there be anything peculiar and interesting about this country?"

At this juncture, Neuhaus recalled the central theme of the conference. "The question, at least in my tangled mind, is Who is the 'we' of 'we the people'? And if politics is about how we ought to order our life together, does law today help or hinder that process, and why, and what may be done about it?"

Silbey followed up on Neuhaus's restatement of the question. "The issue we've been trying to grapple with in this conversation is not whether law creates community. Obviously law can create a community of discourse about the law. At issue is the larger meaning we are attaching to the concept of community. In listening to the conversation one notices that there's a struggle to appropriate the term, that there are different sets of presumptions and claims being attached to it. The notion, by itself, that we are a community, members of a community, does not carry a lot of weight. It makes a claim to authority of a kind that we are not articulating but should articulate. The notion of being a member, of belonging, is part of the moral import that the word *community* is carrying. The question then becomes, If we all wish to be members of some group or multiple groups, what role does a system of rules or sanctions have with regard to membership and multiple membership?"

Law versus Community

"Pastor Neuhaus said that we should focus on the question of whether the law helps or hinders the ordering of our life in the community," noted Gaffney. "That's perhaps intentionally provocative—Richard is good at that sort of thing—but I would take issue with the *or*. I think that it does both, and that that's the problem. To the extent that the law helps community, it helps. To the extent that it impedes and hurts the community, we have to be concerned about that. Law can impede community, and here I am referring expressly to the comments of Professor Berns. For example, the law of liberal democracy tends to reduce the church to the lowest common denominator. It tends to mute the voice of the church precisely as the quid pro quo of having religious freedom or existing in a liberal democracy, and it promotes the relativity of all claims of significance.

"Now, lest that be regarded as too broad, for a second example of law's destructiveness I want to return to the notion that the Enlightenment promise was to end sectarian violence in Europe. But, of course, the radical secularization that was the predicate of that promise didn't yield that result. And the illusion was shattered first in the French Revolution and then in all kinds of other instances in which perfectly enlightened democracies carried on with similar barbarity. It seems to me that the critical point at which these problems of law and ordering a community either have sense or not is when nation-states go to war and engage in massive acts of destruction of life in order to preserve community. When they are willing to do that in the name of preserving the ordering of their lives together, they have reached one of those critical checkpoints at which Tom Shaffer says we have to worry about idolatry. At that point law neither orders life nor creates community; it creates destructive violence. It is coercive, not persuasive. And it coerces with such massive force that we have to question whether liberal democracy is an acceptable means for preserving religious freedom."

Arons then joined the discussion. "I think that there is an unexplored issue here. We have not talked enough about the ways in which the law is destructive of a community. There was a flash point some time back between Professors Shaffer and Berns that we passed over too quickly. I am a little reluctant to return to it, but I am going to do so anyway.

"We were talking about whether so-called liberal democracy has room for particular communities. I don't remember the exact words, but the gist of the exchange was that Professor Shaffer would be willing to subscribe to membership in this liberal democracy provided that it was also possible to pursue those things that are required in the particular community of which he's a member. Professor Berns seemed to respond, 'Well the state will permit you to do that as a matter of grace, but not as a matter of right.' At that point I felt very threatened. It seemed to me that liberal democracy was being depicted as a system in which some people have the power to dispense grace to other people. My first reaction was to be frightened by that. My second reaction was that this is a very convincing argument in favor of the genius of liberal democracy: the tolerance contained in the idea of liberal democracy prevents exactly the kind of battle that might have taken place between these two gentlemen had this been a very large group instead of two people thoughtfully talking to each other.

"So, if tolerance is one of the essences of liberal democracy, then it's necessary to look at the law as a blank screen upon which these various particular peoples attempt to project their morality, their values, whatever. This suggests to me that the essential problem is how to preserve the tolerance that seems to be part of liberal democracy and at the same time engage in a moral discourse without requiring any particular people to abandon themselves or their sense of themselves."

Professor Berns interjected, "May I say something in ten seconds? My point was that we all have to obey the law. No exemptions, on religious grounds, to the law. Five seconds. Second point: throughout most of our history it has been very easy for most religious groups to obey our laws. That's the genius of our laws."

Prophesying about Economics

Bork followed up with a longer intervention. "Most people here have been talking from a religious perspective. I want to talk from a secular perspective, on the side of the claims of the law along the lines that Walter Berns established. Professor Shaffer was talking about the time when the state claims more than it should from the community. I think, however, that his essay and this general discussion are beginning to illustrate a time when the particular community and religion begin to claim more than they should from the state, which also has legitimate claims. And it seems to me, for example, in the discussion of corporate takeovers and what should happen to corporate law when businesses move plants to the Sunbelt, that here religion has rather quickly aligned itself with a particular brand of politics and indeed with a particular set of interest groups. What is illustrated is the inadequacy of major religious premises—their inability, without a lot of worldly knowledge, to know what results they're going to produce in reality.

"In this case, I think the claims made would produce immoral results. For example, Professor Shaffer's paper juxtaposes the notion of profit maximization and the moral and religious claims of the community, which I think is quite wrong. If you're talking about moving plants South, for example, you can be sure that it will inflict some damage on communities in the North. But there will also be costs if plants fail to move South, and these are not even mentioned in this essay. In fact, in a sense, if you believe that all men are brothers, you ought to believe in profit maximization as a motive, because that is the one way to use the resources available in society in a way that benefits most people. I think Professor Shaffer has defined the community much too narrowly, and his analysis and prescription would, outside his narrow community, produce damaging results which are not even taken into account. One ought not to be too quick to translate major moral principles that have been developed without the benefit of a lot of worldly knowledge, a failing I believe the American Catholic bishops exhibited in their economics pastoral."

Shaffer took issue with Bork's remarks. "I framed that argument rather carefully. The bishops' categories are vocation and trust. It isn't that the considerations you mentioned aren't taken into account. It is that the other considerations are also taken into account, as a trustee must take into account all those who are his beneficiaries. Thus, the argument is that the workers in the northern plant, the communities in the North, are as much beneficiaries of the corporate trustee as the investors on Wall Street are."

"I'm not talking about producers," Bork interjected. "I'm talking about consumers, and the workers in the South are not going to get a job if that plant doesn't move."

"Well, I think they too are beneficiaries," Shaffer responded. "Moreover, the destructive force of the law that I see in operation there and in the kind of moral discourse we're talking about is very possibly being overcome with some encouragement from the recent Supreme Court decision countering the argument that the corporate trustee should consider only one constituency. No, the trustee is a trustee for the labor of others, for the capitalists as well as the workers."

Neuhaus entered the exchange between Shaffer and Bork. "I think the point that Robert Bork is making is that in the name of being prophetic, Tom Shaffer's paper is simply pushing a set of utterly predictable left-wing positions that are clearly identifiable on the sociopolitical spectrum and that are already in the public debate. Tomorrow in Washington, D.C., there's going to be a big mobilization against U.S. policy in Central America. It's primarily led by religious groups and a collection of very left-of-center political groups — so left-of-center that the AFL-CIO has dropped out of it. Now, the word *prophetic* is going to be used tomorrow on the steps of the U.S. Capitol, I would be prepared to bet, if I were a betting man, no less than five hundred times in the course of the speeches. They are all going to be there 'prophetically' making pronouncements about what they have discovered within the tradition of their particular peoplehood — that kind of language will be used. The question put by Robert Bork is, Does not your particular people actually represent an instance of acculturation so extreme that it is not even aware of what wells it's drawing from, in terms of the larger culture, and what position it is religionizing and moralizing?"

Frank Alexander of Emory University's School of Law replied to Neuhaus. "That speech just epitomized the dogmatism that you're reacting against. It seems to me that you embodied everything that you now are accusing Professor Shaffer of. You're grasping a double-edged sword. However Professor Shaffer responds, I want you to respond to the same question you are posing to him on any position you take, to see if you can avoid your presumptuousness."

"But I've claimed to be neither a prophet nor a prophet's son nor a seventh son of a prophet's son," responded Neuhaus. "I am not a prophet. I have no prophetic vision whatsoever. As to what our Central American policy should be, for example, I have no word from God."

At this point, Emmerich made two observations. "First, I'd like to say that I feel that there is such a thing as an American community and that law has in fact contributed a great deal to the ordering of that community. Although I don't think this source is exclusive, I personally believe that to a great extent the bond in that community is enunciated in the First Amendment and other provisions of the Bill of Rights. Second, although I did not agree with some aspects of Tom Shaffer's paper, I consider it very thoughtful and very thought provoking. Perhaps it's because I am coming at this issue from a Lutheran, two-kingdoms viewpoint, which is my religious tradition, but I didn't hear the paper saying that this particular people should be a separatist people. Perhaps the fact that he cited Yoder, a Mennonite theologian, may have given some the impression that he believes these people should be separate, but I don't think that's what he's saying. By my reading, he is saying that when you as a Christian in culture are confronted with those issues that make you go to the wall, that's when you have to claim the prophetic voice, if you believe that that's in fact what your religious tradition dictates."

Law and Community, Again

Gerard Bradley of the University of Illinois's College of Law then intervened, bringing up once again the law-community issue. "I have two things I want to mention about how law can be constructive or destructive of community. One is a comparison of the way two similar cases are treated in law. One of the cases is current and the other one occurred 150 years ago. The older case took place in New York, where somebody named Ruggles stated in some public square that Christ was a bastard and his mother must have been a whore. Well, the community was not too pleased with the statement, and he was prosecuted for blasphemy. Now, the judge was Chancellor Kent of New York State Court. His reasoning is interesting. You might have expected him or someone like him to say, Well that's obviously false and therefore you just can't say such a thing. But the judge said, Whether or not what you say is true, whether or not it's false, doesn't matter. It's a grave offense to the moral sensibilities of the community, and we're not going to let you say it. Ruggles was convicted of blasphemy. Now—and this is going back to the point Pastor Neuhaus made this morning about whether there's more consensus now than there was then on certain issues—I think that there's much more conformity in our society now than there was 150 years ago, probably more consensus about most things. We are certainly a more homogeneous society. But now, if you would take these same phenomena, the case could come out in directly the opposite manner. Not because consensus has changed but because now the legal analysis treats a community's moral consensus as the bogeyman. The consensus is oppressive because the object of legal analysis, as well as liberal sympathies, is the dissenting individual. The final moral of the story, I guess, is that there may be the stuff of community out there that is in consensus about some very important things, but the legal system refracts that in a destructive way such that, in fact, the consensus in the community is what the law protects us against.

"The second point is about the privatization of religion that is going on in American society. The law would like religion to be completely privatized and to a great extent is trying to privatize it. I think one of the reasons law is doing that is because religion is a competitor in the prescription of public norms. I think the law tries to privatize religion for the same reason it shies away from using terms like *truth*. The legal community, the culture at large, and mass media don't call things *true*, they call them *preferences*, and *values*, and *interests*. You have an 'interest' in believing in God. Well, I don't know what that means. There may be good reasons for this kind of discourse, and I think that Tom Shaffer may have mentioned some of them. However, a history of 1,500 years in which religion has often been responsible for bloodletting is something that has to be treated very carefully. I think that's the major culturally available argument against public religion—that if you let the genie out of the bottle it will be like

Tudor England or something like that. The point is that we should recover a vocabulary of truth which may lead us to talk more intelligently about community."

Burtchaell followed Bradley. He began with a quip about the use of the word *we* by several participants in the conference. "Listening to the conversation that Professor Shaffer has inspired, I've been reminded of the old joke about the Lone Ranger and Tonto being surrounded by a group of hostile Indians. As the Indians close in, the Lone Ranger says, 'It looks like we're in trouble, Tonto!' And Tonto says, 'Who is this "we"?' I've been wondering the same thing throughout much of our conversation: Who is this 'we'?

"I am convinced that Tom Shaffer is a deceiver, a trickster. The hands are the hands of Yoder, but the voice is the voice of Shaffer. Tom learned from the Anabaptist's sense of truculence about his citizenship, but he is not a consistent elaborator of it as an Anabaptist. He's acting as a Catholic, and that's who I am too. Now, from that point of view, truculence pursued, how is it that the law seems right now to be so unresponsive in helping us frame a more constructive society? I think that this is what Tom has been leading us to see.

"American society has a moral discourse, a vibrant moral discourse, with eventual legal results in which, increasingly, active participants come from communities whose most resonant sources of moral insight are their shared religious faiths. This is true now in a way that was not so much the case earlier. Now, opposed to these truculent people, who like Shaffer are more active than retiring, is a powerful and influential alliance of people who despise and exclude any contributions that are religiously oriented or phrased. They regard such contributions as private, as authoritatively imposed and therefore not sincere or autonomous. To them it is all priestcraft and dogma. These people, if I understand them correctly, insist that public moral discourse has to be framed only in shared terms, and since they veto all religious discourse as inappropriate to the public square, especially the one right in front of the U.S. Capitol, they have in fact seized a veto power over the terms of the public moral discourse which is the fount of much law. And yet they continue to demand quite a bit of reverence for their own axioms and their own sages, which others might be inclined to characterize as their own dogmas and saints. As it works out, anyone who doesn't share their dogmas and saints can't participate fully in the public discourse that affects the law. We have been handicapped and hobbled.

"The Americans whose vision of a better society and whose zeal for better law arises from their communities of faith right now encounter two special frustrations. The state, because of the enlargement of its funding power, is involved as a controlling partner with an enormous matrix of institutions which are crucially important in the formation of conviction and understanding in our society in a way that was not so before the New Deal. This newly activist state, through its funding power, controls as a virtual monopoly institutions by which these convictions are influenced. And it excludes from them, as not germane to their task, the whole world of moral discourse which previously was considered legitimate in those institutions. These same people, in a view which to us is naive but quite steel-like and determined, have made their institutions the carriers of what many are coming to recognize as dogma, and they have excluded the counterproposals and counterviews of their fellow citizens."

Wrapping Up

Toward the end of the second session of the conference, Shaffer was given the last word. "I've already imposed on you too long. Having something I wrote be talked about so well, so long, by so many people I admire is humbling. Thank you very much. I don't know why we don't have this sort of discourse in university law schools, though I don't know of anybody who's vetoing it in the sense that Jim Burtchaell talks about public discourse being vetoed or restricted. All I have to say about that is that it's not my fault.

"I wanted to pick up on the law-in-Israel question that Harold Berman raised at the beginning. He asked, Where is the law in Israel when I speak of the law in Canaan? I think that's a very perceptive critique, and what I want to say about it is that the law in Israel is not coercive. Someone said that tolerance is of the essence of liberal democracy. It is also of the essence of biblical morals. Now, in the West, which is simply another way to state my problem about Constantine, we have to say that moral discourse—the law in Israel, if you like—is no longer coercive.

That is true of internal governance within the particular people, and it's also true of the formulation of the moral witness it will make in the broader community.

"I understand us as participating fully and with hope in the larger community. I think that's true of modern polity even within the Catholic Church. I use Yoder here because Yoder describes it well, particularly in an essay with the horrible title 'The Hermeneutic of Peoplehood.' There is a model for it in St. Paul—it's the seventh chapter of 1 Corinthians. It's in that spirit that the particular people conducts its polity and formulates its arguments in the larger community. Now, there are some differences in the way these arguments are presented.

"The reason I use the Roman Catholic bishops' letter is because the bishops seem to me to make the broadest formulation, with the broadest spectrum of moral argument, within the broader society. I used that letter not because I wanted to make a Roman Catholic argument but because it is a broad example from a group of people who frankly admit, right at the beginning, that they regard American democratic society pragmatically. It is a medium for communication as far as they are concerned. They don't buy into anybody's system, and they make that very clear. One can also cite some Jewish sources.

"If I were going to explore these questions specifically as a Catholic, as an American Catholic, I would want to pay a lot more attention to the immigrants—not only the Catholic immigrants since about 1850 but the Jewish immigrants as well. The late immigrants in American society were not a part of the historic American vision, and it's not clear to me that they were ever fully brought into it. Their real lives were centered on interpersonal associations, or at least that's what I get from the story, so that on the question that Professor Silbey raised, they know what a community is and they remember what a community is. There's my corporate executive, that's who I was talking about—she remembers what a community is, and that's what she wants to build.

"As far as the question about who is this 'we,' I think that the religious tradition has an interesting contribution to make in its understanding that the community is tragic. I take it to be fundamental sociology that a community is defined by whom it excludes. That means that a community is fundamentally tragic. The religious tradition knows how to live with that. It doesn't live with it without pain, but it knows how to live with it. You see it with church struggles over homosexuality, for example. Simone Weil said she was entirely convinced by the New Testament and wanted to become a Christian, but when she looked at all the people the churches kept out, she decided that Jesus would be with them, so she didn't join up. That's what I mean. I wonder, really, if liberal democracy is equal to that kind of truth. I don't know that it is.

"Finally, on prophetic witness. I am willing to take some other phrase for that after all the heat I've gotten." But it was heat, most would agree, that also generated some light.

BEYOND DUTIES AND RIGHTS

At the beginning of the third session of the conference, Neuhaus made a brief introduction recalling the central theme and praising Stith's innovative paper. "If you'll forgive my repetition, I'd like to note again my premise that politics is the rational deliberation of how we ought to order our lives together, my assumption that law is part of politics, and my question of whether law today is contributing and/or hindering that big project, and why. Now, Richard Stith takes us through a very interesting exercise, and we're going to have to make a decision somewhere along here, playing it by ear, as to how much we want to become embroiled and enmeshed in his elegant work with respect to the rights-obligation rationale. Stith's work, which I find very intriguing indeed, moves us toward the proposition that there are duties that do not fit the correlativity hypothesis. Behind that, of course, is an issue evident in the other essays as well: Are we to talk about living law or are we to talk about law and the dynamics of reciprocal behavior patterns that are beyond the bounds of formal law? All of that is closely related to this notion of the duty of generosity.

"As you know, ethics, with respect to rights and duties, is very often discussed in terms of discovery or invention. Classically stated, whether in terms of the Mosaic law or in terms of natural law or whatever, there is a tradition that suggests that we discover right and wrong. Somewhere it is given in nature or given by God and then it is a task of human beings to discover it. As Susan Silbey reminded us, the first way of going about such things is to push the law to mirror what it is that we have discovered to be morally true. With the Enlightenment project, people more or less despaired of discovering any 'extrinsic moral truth' and therefore moved from discovery to invention.

"I take Richard Stith's fascinating paper to be an exercise in turning the Enlightenment against itself. That is, he's in the invention mode, and is exploring whether in fact precisely in the mode of invention you do not discover, paradoxically enough, that there is something that cannot be explained, something that, in fact, is constitutive of what makes law such a critical part of the ordering of our life together. So I find it an intellectually engaging enterprise in which Richard is engaged, and I hope in our discussion we will ask if we find it persuasive. What would it mean, what kind of things should be done, to move toward an understanding of law that is, as the late Robert Coven liked to say, the law of obligation rather than the law of rights? I'm not sure where all that goes, but that's why we're all here, to find out."

A Duty to Rescue

After Neuhaus's introduction, Stith summarized his paper and Berns promptly began the discussion. "Richard Stith, when I first read your paper, I remembered vaguely a law that seemed to fit your case rather well. I appeal to the legal historians here to be precise about it, but I believe it involved a formal rule of law that one had a kind of neighborly duty, for example, to remove a fire hazard from a neighbor's house; failure to do so could be punished. It was an old rule that fell afoul of the modern notion of the busybody or something like that. Now, wouldn't that fit this case rather well?"

Next in line, Glendon commented, "This idea of affirmative duty, of generosity, of rescue, or of aid for your neighbor is characteristic of civil law, not of common law. And if I may, it seems to me that we've been speaking of the Enlightenment as setting the framework for this rights discourse without being sufficiently discriminating about branches of the Enlightenment on just this sort of point.

"Enlightenment thought has very different implications for law, depending upon whether you're talking about the branch that includes Hobbes, Locke, Bentham, Austin, Holmes, or the branch that begins with Rousseau's critique of Hobbes, which had a very strong effect on the civil law system. It seems to me that in this room when we've talked about the Enlightenment we've had in mind a set of thoughts, traceable to Hobbes, about strict separation between law and justice, about law as a command of the sovereign, backed up by force, and about the individual, as Tom Shaffer said yesterday, radically alone with his rights. In Europe, especially as the Enlightenment affected the legal system in the great codifications of the eighteenth century, there were other attitudes which as undercurrents strongly modified those propositions. Montesquieu kept alive the idea of custom, which was pretty well rooted out of our system by the time of Holmes. Holmes didn't even mention it when he listed the sources of law, statutes cases, and so on. Rousseau's critique of Hobbes kept alive as an undercurrent the classical idea of law as, among other things, persuasion as well as coercion and as leading toward virtue. So, when we speak of rights, I think we have to distinguish between a particularly exaggerated form of rights discourse that goes on in the United States and other ways in which rights discourse can be imagined in other types of liberal democracies." For example, she continued, in the United States we speak about the rights of women and the rights of the unborn. European countries have not framed their discussion of abortion that way.

Stith asked Glendon for a clarification. "In Europe do duties to rescue correlate with claim rights as they do here in the U.S.?"

Glendon referred the question to Berman. "Well, it is essentially in criminal law," said Berman, "that there is a duty to rescue. Actually it worked out in practice very much the way our law does. Our judges sometimes talk in immoral or amoral terms and say there's no duty, but our law imposes duties, quite often, and this leads me to say something which I think is relevant on the comparative level and relevant also to our broader discussion. We have philosophies about law of the kind that Professor Glendon has mentioned and which we've all talked about. Holmes is an example of this. If you look at what the judges are doing in our law, we have a much more communal system of law in many respects than the Europeans may have, even though they talk in other philosophical terms. For example, the Germans have had in the nineteenth and twentieth centuries this great historical jurisprudence: law grows out of history, and so forth. Meanwhile they have a code system in which the courts are looking at the code. We have positivism and natural-law theory, but our courts are operating with a historical approach, looking back at the precedents and so on and so forth. Our law imposes high moral duties. A lot of what Professor Stith has talked about is embodied in our law. For example, in the law of trusts, the trustee has a duty to act in favor of the beneficiary of the trust, a duty to be more concerned, more solicitous for the beneficiary than he would be for himself. I think that it's very helpful to have this analytical exploration of generosity and what Lon Fuller called the morality of aspiration, which is very hard to enforce at all."

Glendon replied: "The topic of our conference is law and the ordering of our life together, and with that in mind, I think we have to distinguish between what's going on in the capillaries of the legal system, of which only specialists are generally aware, and what is highly visible to everyone. It is true that one can find the language of duty and morality at the level of principle, but this is not the case at the operational level. I am thinking about the first year of law school, when the torts professor horrifies you by saying, 'Well, suppose there's a swimming pool and a little five-year-old girl is drowning in there, and there are twelve Olympic swimmers sitting around who could rescue her with no risk to themselves at all. Do they have to do anything?' And of course you all say 'Yes, of course they have to jump right in.' 'Wrong, wrong,' says the professor gleefully. It is important that at the level of principle one legal system says they must rescue and they will be criminally punished if they don't, and the other says they don't have to. What I'm suggesting is that our legal system, for historical reasons, has made it very difficult to talk about the things that are most important to us as a society, except in the rather impoverished language of rights sheared off from duties, which are characteristically paired with rights in the civil-law system."

To Start with Rights or to Start with the Good

"I take this to be an essay in moral philosophy more than anything else," said Martin Golding. "I'm trying to locate the problem that is bothering Professor Stith and a lot of other people who have written about rights discourse, myself included. I think that the fundamental issue is the extent to which our moral relations can be formulated in terms of the language of rights and duties and the extent to which they cannot. My own feeling is that in recent years there has been a move in moral philosophy toward what they call rights-based ethical systems. One of the features of those systems is a prominent individualism. In the debate between those who think that the language of rights and duties is crucial and everything else is peripheral and those who disagree with that, I think that the crucial question is where one starts from in justifying a moral claim. Do we start out on the Hobbesian side, where all obligation is self-obligation? In other words, do we start out with me—what is owed to me and so on—and then move on to you, to a consideration of your rights, which leads us to the conclusion that I owe nothing unless I oblige myself? Do you start out that way? Or do you start out from the other end and ask what is the good of the other person, what duties do I therefore have, and the like?

"I think that's the crucial difference—whether you start out with a notion of liberty in which all obligation and duty involve kinds of self-limitation or whether you start out with some welfare notion in which all duty and rights derive somehow from the good of the other and of oneself. That's the crucial issue in this whole debate over the status of rights in moral discourse. My own feeling is that the language of morality has become very legalized in recent years—that is, moral discourse has become very legal in its procedures, in the way it argues and so on."

At this point, Mary Segers of Rutgers University focused on abortion and law. "I am not a law professor or a lawyer, so my comments are very different. At the end of the paper, when Professor Stith comes to the abortion question, he's concerned with the law as a teacher. That made me think to myself, Well, if the law is to teach, it should teach accurately and well. The analogy he used was that of the smoker. You tolerate the smoker because the smoker somehow is driven by an inner compulsion to smoke. So I thought, Is that really analogous to the woman in the abortion situation? An involuntarily pregnant woman faced with an abortion dilemma may not be driven by some sort of inner compulsion. Actually, the law might seem rather paternalistic in its view of her: Poor thing, she's doing the wrong thing but can't help it, so we'll excuse her. It occurred to me that the abortion situation is really much more determined by external circumstances of poverty or rape or incest or abandonment or whatever, and my general concern is how the law is going to teach about women in this situation. I would be concerned about any approach that sees the pedagogical function of the law as central. I would be concerned that the law would teach well about women as well as the importance of life, the value of unborn life.

"My other comment is about a book by Carol Gilligan on the language of rights versus a language of care. That book has probably been misunderstood and even greatly overrated. She explicitly says she did not link the language of rights and the language of care in any gender-specific way, and yet the content of the book seems to suggest that she does. There are some interesting discussions of Gilligan by some feminists who question very seriously the origin of this language of care and who note that the language of care seems to be enunciated by people who are in relatively vulnerable, powerless situations. In the abortion issue that Gilligan analyzes, the women were somehow deferring, picking up signals from the people to whom they felt responsible and toward whom they felt duties, because they were in relatively powerless situations. Joan Tronto, a political philosopher at Hunter College, has done a careful analysis of Gilligan's work to pinpoint the social situations in which this language of care arises, this ethic of responsibility. If this ethic arises in situations among, say, blacks and other marginalized, oppressed groups in society, if the language of care is arising from situations in which people feel relatively powerless, that should make us think a little bit more about duties of care and generosity."

The Notion of Neighbor

Burtchaell shifted the focus of the discussion to Stith's buffer-zone concept. "The buffer zone, as you describe it, deals with marginally valuable things, not centrally valuable things. But the margin, as I understand it, grows thicker as mutual commitment expands. It is definitely a function of a variable relationship between the parties. It requires bilateral trust. It isn't just a factual matter, and it isn't just a matter of what each person senses as duty. There has to be what I would call an obligation rather than a debt. It's not that I owe someone something but rather that I sense that I have a bond toward that person. This, I think, is what we meant when we were talking about community earlier—that I consider these other persons not as strangers but as neighbors. It was so striking to hear talk about neighbors, because we don't know what neighbors are in America or, indeed, in open society. I think that when we talk about a deferential attitude, it's not a matter of an attitude based on another's claim but of an attitude based upon one's own sense of determination to behave in a certain way.

"One of the infections from legal language back into moral language has been the understanding that we serve one another's needs because of those needs. A claim originates in the neighbor's need that goes beyond right. But I think that the situation is better understood in terms of my binding myself to the other person not because the other person gets a grab on me but because I need to be the kind of person who cannot ignore another's needs. The reason I must jump into the pool, though I can hardly swim, is that if I watch the child die I have estranged the child from me and something worse in me has died than in the child. Now this, of course, is virtue language. Richard Stith is trying to find duties that are not generated by rights in the other person and to move from there to a notion that is wider and probably deeper too. But it seems to me that he has to be very careful about using the language of duties, dues, or debts, that he might want to choose a language reflecting the idea that virtue is generated from within the agent, from within the actor."

"You say that if you let the child die you would have a hard time living with yourself because something would happen to you, you would lose if you let the child die?" Neuhaus asked Burtchaell.

"I would wither," said Burtchaell.

"You would wither, you would be lessened by this," said Neuhaus. "This then is a relationship in which you acknowledge mutual dependency with this child."

"No," said Burtchaell. "Even if they let me drown, I will not let them drown. I can only really form community on any long-term basis with others who reciprocate that, it is true. But the bond cannot come simply from the reciprocity. It has to come from the fact that each of us, within ourselves, knows that we are bound to the other."

"But that's what I'm getting at," said Neuhaus. "You are bound to the others, so it's not a one-way kind of virtuous altruistic action on your part."

"Yes it is," Burtchaell insisted. "I bind myself to them because of *my* utter need. I cannot survive without being their servant in their need."

"Why?" asked Neuhaus. "Because of your nature in relation to God, creation, covenant?"

"Because of my nature, period," Burtchaell answered.

Neuhaus asked yet another question. "Ah, well, what's the philosophy of human nature predicated on? At least I think that's the kind of question Stith's argument raises."

"It is based upon the cumulative experience of a community," Burtchaell replied, "in my case the Christian community. But it is not a statement about Christians. It is a statement about human beings. Human beings who stand by and watch others drown will themselves die spiritually. The obligation arises from within myself, toward others."

At this point, Berns confronted Burtchaell with a hypothetical situation based on the biblical story of the Good Samaritan. "Put yourself on the road from Jerusalem to Jericho approaching someone who's fallen by the roadside. Say you're a priest, if not a Levite. What is the nature of your obligation?"

"Well, the priest and the Levite died," said Burtchaell. "They got to Jericho, but they were dead within when they got there. The Samaritan arrived the poorer of purse and yet flourishing within. That, I think, is the point.

"It seems to me that among mutually caring people, talk of enforcement is a sign that there has been a collapse. I live in a religious community that has a written rule. If ever there is talk of enforcement and not simply of reminding, of calling one another to the obligation that they willingly undertook, then we are in a state of collapse. Of course the good thing about legally enforceable rights is that it allows people who do not enjoy community to live in a moderately peaceable society."

Gaffney brought the discussion back to the central theme of the conference. "I want to get to Richard Neuhaus's reference to the overarching question of our conference—Does law assist or hinder the ordering of our life together? My opinion is that it does both. It both helps and hinders. It depends on what kind of community we're talking about, to be sure, but it also depends on what kind of formal legal structures we're talking about.

"First of all, I want to suggest how the law hinders the ordering of our life together on this very point of a duty of assistance. I'm not a tort professor, but perhaps those who are will jump in and correct whatever errors I make. As I understand it, the law imposes, or has imposed in several cases that I'm aware of, civil liability for good-faith attempts to help. The net effect of that kind of law is to motivate people to avoid getting involved, to avoid giving serious attention to what Richard Stith is talking about.

"On the other hand, our American law does center on the notion of the duty of judicial compassion. Someone objected earlier to the prospect of there being no restraints on the judiciary if morality is the 'open sesame' of whatever a judge can do. But if we limit the duty of judicial compassion to the kind of reinforcement of participation in the community that we find in the situations of groups that have historically been excluded from participation through voting rules and the like, then it might behoove the judge to be judicially activist in the name of care for those who have been excluded from the community. In any event, I think that it is fair to say that American law both helps and hinders the ordering of our life together along the lines of duty rather than rights analysis that Richard Stith has suggested."

Manners and Morals

Shaffer also commented on Stith's paper. "Well, I take this paper to be primarily an exercise in moral philosophy of virtue. And I think this exploration of manners is really interesting, really clever. The focus, it seems to me, might be this: What do I want for the other? It seems to me that the virtue answer to that is, I want the other to be good, as opposed to right in the sense of having rectitude, and as opposed to free in the sense of autonomy or self-rule. If that's so, if that's the question and that's the answer from a virtue perspective, then we've got to be careful about using the manners strategy. I am as attracted to manners as you are, but I think that the purpose of manners is to make the other person comfortable."

"As opposed to good?" Neuhaus asked.

"Yes, well, actually there's kind of a selfish edge to it too," said Shaffer. "I want the other to be comfortable so I'll be comfortable. When I look at the virtue of generosity through the lens of manners, I see a contrast there between a description of generosity that offers the other the same moral gain I see for myself and a description of generosity that assumes that the other lacks the discipline that I have.

"I want to make another point about that. I wonder if generosity doesn't tend to depend on rights. In the examples you use, generosity assumes a kind of equal starting point. If there was only one cookie on the plate, and those of us in this corner had been eating cookies for a while, and Frank came in and hadn't had any cookies yet, we would all want him to have this cookie. It would become his cookie because of some distributive assumption in this business about leaving the last cookie, which really is a matter of right. That seems to me even more important with regard to the buffer zone. I wonder if this is right: It's only possible to have a buffer zone when there's a clear idea about where the line is. For one thing, that will tell us where the buffer zone has to be, and it may tell us how wide it has to be. And then, from time to time, we're going to have to allude to the line. In legal terms, we're going to have to allude to the line when the property changes hands."

Bork jumped in at this point. "I agree with the major premise of this paper, that we have a society which has too many rights claims in it. I know because sometimes I have to listen to what I regard as legally sound but nonetheless trivial claims of rights. The constant claim to rights is enormously polarizing in all kinds of other institutions. By putting law inside institutions and defining rights, we have split people apart. In some sense, I think the revival of the doctrine of standing is a way of getting around that. Having said that, however, I'm afraid that I can think of no examples of anything called a duty in which there is not a correlative right, and that includes the examples Professor Stith has offered. I don't think it matters what language you use. If there's a primitive society in which there is no word for right, when somebody comes and says that a wrong has been done, that person is in effect saying, I have a claim, in some sense, with regard to something that needs to be rectified. And that is an assertion of a right.

"The confusion stems, I think, from our moving from a level of etiquette or manners or morals to law. We talk about a duty, a duty of etiquette, and then say there is no correlative right. On the contrary, I think there is a correlative right in every one of the cases that Richard Stith gives. I can think of no example in which there is anything called a duty that is interactive in any sense in which there is not a correlative right. Take for example the situation in which A may have a right to drive B out of business and Professor Stith says that B has no duty to close the shop. That's not an accurate statement of the situation. The fact of the matter is that A has a right to compete in certain ways which may ultimately drive B out of business, and B has a duty not to interfere with A's behaving in those ways: there is the correlative duty and right. I'm sorry. I like your major thesis and I share your uneasiness about the constant claim of rights in our society, but I don't think that this breaking apart of duty and right does it."

A Scarcity of Moral Capital

Bradley then entered the discussion. "I'd like to address Harold Berman about his earlier remark about the reality of social interrelations. To some extent I think he is saying that the reality of legal practice is much more moral or more communal than our thinking about it and our language for discussing it are. My concern is that while that may be true, to the extent that it is true, it's because we're still living off accumulated capital from another time, and I think that Professor Berman might agree that this phenomenon is rooted in the historical nature of legal inquiry. But that diminishes the severity of the crisis only a little, because there are forces loose which are going to keep using up the capital that we may have accumulated at an earlier time.

"Rights talk is destructive of a valuable way of ordering our life together. It has little appreciation of communities, analyzing as it does conflictual situations between individuals and other corporate bodies, for the most part. There is really very little break built into legal analysis in this respect. I think Richard Stith's is a plaintive cry to reintegrate into conventional legal discourse a vocabulary and/or modes of analysis which allow for community to a larger extent. I don't think our legal discourse does that, and the courts have very little appreciation of the need to do that.

"You see that in families. We're in a process of individualizing family relationships for the most part. That is, husbands and wives are more and more treated as litigants. They're basically treated like strangers, and the state is losing the sense that to intervene in that social relationship is really qualitatively different from intervening in relationships among strangers. What I am concerned about is how you can have the legal tradition restrain itself with its own resources when I don't really see those resources or the desire for restraint."

Neuhaus reiterated Bradley's question to Berman. "Harold, I'd like you to respond to the suggestion that maybe you're right when you say that the practice of law is better than the philosophy and the analysis of law, but the philosophy and the analysis and the language are consuming whatever redeeming elements there are in practice, which are basically the moral capital of the past."

"Yes, I wanted to say something about that," Berman responded. "I think that it's true that our law is becoming uprooted from tradition. Law is using up this enormous capital which it was given in a conception of law which goes back to biblical times—the law as part of the covenant between God and his people. The Western European legal tradition owes much to the Judeo-Christian tradition as well as the Greco-Roman tradition. Our conception of law derives from those roots, and in spite of all the ensuing philosophical changes that took place during the Enlightenment and so forth, I think it's really only in the twentieth century that there has been a kind of uprooting. I think it has come with the world wars and a host of other things.

"It bothers me when philosophers and jurists, speaking in the abstract about law, say, Well law is this and law is that. They tend to demean it, tend to narrow it, tend to think that laws are incompatible with morals or independent of morals. And then you have to say, On the other hand, or No, that is not our legal tradition. Our legal tradition grew up with the closest bond not only between law and morals but between law and faith, law and the whole conception of the universe and so forth. There is a tendency to adopt certain theories about law that make it deal with the mean side of human nature and cut it off from these other connections. That's when I say, No, it's not necessarily so; the tradition is very different; and the tradition is that law and morals reinforce each other historically.

"The historical thing is, I think, the critical factor, because philosophy without history is empty. What we're all really talking about is what historical moment we're at, and the time is ripe now to say these things. I agree absolutely with Gerard Bradley when he says that we're living off this accumulated capital. I don't think we're going to get to a sense of the future without recapturing this very rich legal tradition which is still a lot of our law."

Buzzard then spoke on the relationship between law and virtue. "The issue of the relationship between law and virtue takes us back to Pastor Neuhaus's fundamental question about how law is going to help us and to Dr. Berman's comment about law perhaps having more links to morality than some people are prepared to recognize. That gets us into theological and jurisprudential questions about the educative role of law and even what we mean by law. It seems to me that there's a lot of confusion about what law can and can't do about moral questions. In some areas we see the law quite prepared to introduce those questions. In some ways law has become a vehicle for discourse about morality in civil rights, employment areas, and capital punishment. We see law as a vehicle for moral conversation in those areas. I think people do tend to look to law for some guidance about fundamental moral questions. On the other hand, we've had a conversation here about rights orientation creating some limits to law's capacity to speak clearly on moral issues; about our pluralism—or our asserted diversity, anyway—as interfering with that; and about the loss of other structures in our society that carry some of the moral freight.

"The question that haunts me as a lawyer, as a professor, as someone interested in our culture, is where we are to look in our culture for moral instruction (and not moral instruction simply to small communities, which may go on or may not). Where do we look for a conversation, in the culture, about moral principles? As government has dominated more and more of our society and is more nervous, in some regards, about moral conversation, one wonders if the conversation is going to go on."

Last Words

Stith concluded this session of the conference. "In the little time I have left here, I'd like to respond to three people: Robert Bork, Tom Shaffer, and Mary Segers.

"I really would not concede your point, Robert Bork, that there are duties without rights. Even on the superficial level, I would describe duty differently. The duty is to give the cookie to the person who takes it and not to resent that. Now, sure, if that keeps happening, then there will be some resentment. But I think in the first instance there is a sense of true generosity without any upset or call for sanctions against the person. And even if there are sanctions, as there might be after repeated grabs for cookies, they are still on a different level. I'm not trying to do an anthropological study to point out that human communities exist without ever making demands on their members.

"Tom Shaffer, I thought, was right on the money when he pointed out some of the deep moral and metaphysical inadequacies that I alluded to briefly in the essay.

"I want to respond to Mary Seger's point because I think it raises the larger issues of abortion and paternalism. You wouldn't like the West German abortion position, because it really is saying that it is necessary to educate women in the duties of motherhood. It's the paternalistic idea that we train the parents in their duty. Now, I have a lot of sympathy for that, but I think that's a real problem in terms of mediating structures. My ultimate notion of a good society is a socialist society in which all of us take responsibility for everyone else's needs and well-being and justice. But it would have to operate through mediating structures, not through the state doing everything; each subordinate level would have to be trained regarding its appropriate virtues."

THE LAW AND THE FAMILY

The final session opened with Bruce Hafen of Brigham Young University's J. Reuben Clark Law School reviewing his essay and with Golding initiating the discussion. "Professor Hafen understands freedom of expression in two senses—as a negative right and a positive right," said Golding. "The notion of negative rights is, 'Don't interfere with me; I can believe what I want.' The notion of positive rights is, 'I really have a claim I can make against you to supply me with something good.' That is, I think, a distinction that we have overlooked. Negative freedom and positive freedom weren't emphasized enough, so that when it comes to, say, the abortion issue, a lot of the confusion in the discussion using rights terms stems from a failure to distinguish rights in these different senses. Then, once it's conceded that there is a right as an immunity from interference on the part of government, publicists and even lawyers, who probably should know better, jump to the conclusion that if there's a right, then the state also has to supply the individual with the means to enjoy that right."

Sanford Katz of Boston College School of Law spoke next. "Both in our law and in practice I think that there is what I would call a romantic or idealized vision of the nature of the family. I think that the Supreme Court, particularly, has a romantic notion of the family without a clue as to its reality. In the law there is no such thing as the family, unlike a corporation or a union. It is assumed to be a constellation of human relations. At the same time that there has been an emphasis on individual rights in the form of civil rights for minorities, women, and children, there has also been, in family law, an emphasis on individual rights, on protecting individuals. For example, the abortion decision mentioned earlier is, as I read it, a protection of an individual's right— a woman's right—to have an abortion if she chooses. At the same time, there is child liberation—a child's right to be educated, a child's right to sue his parents, a child's right to do this, to do that. Again, this has been championed by the liberal establishment as if this bandwagon of civil rights is or has an end result that is desirable.

"I want to ask Bruce Hafen about the extent to which the movement of protecting individual rights in the husband-wife and parent-child relationships is interfering with the social idea of the family as an association of human beings sharing values in a traditional family structure. To what extent is Robert Bork right in saying that the emphasis on individual rights is polarizing the family?"

Hafen responded, "I think it's important to remember that one of the reasons there has been such a movement to intervene in discretionary relationships is that they had been so widely abused. Part of our history going way back is an attempt to redress the terrible injuries that resulted from improperly used patriarchal authority, not only in families but in all kinds of relationships. In some sense the movement of individual liberty is an attempt to throw off all of those chains. I see the value of that because of child abuse and spouse abuse and all of the other things that take place there. It's understandable to me that there would be attempts to seek redress."

Neuhaus interjected a question and a comment. "Are you really content to say what you just said—that the reason for formal-law interventions in the family and in other mediating structures is the abuse that has taken place within them? Because there's no evidence for that. Interventions are taking place now in a way that they were not fifty or one hundred years ago. There's no evidence that the abuse is greater today than it was fifty or one hundred years ago. So why is this happening now? It's not because of the abuse within those institutions, is it?"

"Ironically, one of the things that interests me about the current state of family law is that at the same time you have intervention, you have an increasing resistance to intervention in the name of resisting the state," said Hafen. "So that the standards for abuse in parent-child relationships have, in some ways, been raised. Even as there's more intervention, in some ways the state has to meet a higher burden. You can't intervene because of the *appearance* of moral neglect, for instance. There has to be more evidence than that."

A Reconstructed Family?

At this point Stephen Arons joined the discussion by recalling Katz's comments. "I think that Mr. Katz was probably correct in his observation about the possibility that individual rights claims are polarizing and alienating the family. I wonder whether this polarizing—and perhaps even alienating—phase that you make reference to might simply be a way station along the path of reconstructing the family, at least from some people's point of view. Here we might be looking at the point at which various communities or mediating structures are reconceptualizing or reconstructing themselves. There's a natural kind of fear when that is going on, as if you were leaping from one cliff to another and in that instant when you're between the two you look down and realize that it's all quite miraculous, that you could just as easily fall through the middle as make it to the other side. This process of change is rather discomfiting, but we may feel, some years from now, after we've reached the other side, that this was endurable in the first place. What we're looking at, I think, is a moment in which the family is being reconstructed from the bottom up rather than from the top down, and that may be upsetting to people who liked or were accustomed to the way it was before. The rights claims have basically deconstructed the family as we knew it. That doesn't mean, however, that there is no family or that our present sense of loss about that will not eventually be compensated by something else."

Katz went on to make some additional comments on the prevalence of individual rights in family matters. "I hate to bring up the Baby M case, but it's an illustration of a trend toward self-gratification. The justification goes like this: 'If I want to be artificially inseminated as a woman—if I get gratification out of that— then I will be inseminated regardless of what my husband wants. If I want to have a baby outside our marriage, I will have the baby outside our marriage because I want it and that's part of my rights outside the normal human relation that we usually think of as family.' Another indication of the prevalence of individual rights is that in the publicity surrounding the Baby M case, which dominated this country's media for weeks, there was never mention of the question of what family Baby M belongs to. It was always a question of which of Mary Beth's or someone else's rights were involved, never a question of family rights. I think that reflects a collapse in culture."

Gerard Bradley followed up on Katz's comment. "Whatever visible form the family may take in the future, I think it will be produced by egocentric analyses of family obligations and relations. The biggest demands that are made on marriage in this culture at this time center on the idea that marriage is an association of individuals for primarily individual purposes."

"Do you think that egocentricity is on the rise in our society largely because other things are on the wane?" asked Arons.

"Well, let's take the Baby M case, for instance," said Bradley. "The one thing about the recent Vatican instruction on procreation that really struck me is that, in contrast with the publicity about the Baby M case, the Vatican was basically saying that no one has a right to a child and that therefore an infertile couple, for instance, may have to endure the sadness of being childless. I think that Professor Katz is quite right in saying that our society's thinking is quite different than the Vatican's. Our society believes that one has a right to a child because the child will gratify personal desire. Our society does not see a child as a gift from God which God can withdraw or withhold."

Arons remarked, "I think that things like the Baby M case arise because we have so much difficulty locating ourselves with regard to an explainable past and an unpredictable future."

Neuhaus entered the exchange between the two professors. "There's a symbiotic relationship between intervention on the one hand and the ideology of self-satisfaction on the other. In other words, one reinforces the other. I would only add, Professor Arons, that you have used the word *oppression*."

"From the perspective of people who prefer family as a sacred covenant and not as a formalistic contract, the oppression is being perpetrated by the assault of this hostile ideology of self-satisfaction against what they believe they have a right to," Arons responded. "And when the law takes the side of the child in the name of children's rights, or whatever, in many cases the parents feel that an act of injustice or oppression has been committed against them: the relationship into which they had entered covenantally, with all kinds of reasonable expectations reinforced by venerable tradition, is now being violated by ideologists employing state power.

"I would, by the way, like to add that I don't think the condition of the family, the bad condition of the family now, can be attributed simply to the intervention of rights."

Professor Mary Segers added, "I'm not so sure that the bad state of the family, whether it's attributable to ideologically hostile forces attacking it or what have you, isn't simply a result of large-scale demographic changes in society. For example, there have been declining fertility rates since the nineteenth century. Also there has been increased participation of women in the labor force, from ten percent in the year 1900 to a much higher percentage today. Whatever large-scale changes are going on, the law begins to reflect them. When we talk about changes in customs or changes in family relations, surely we can't view them in isolation from such large-scale social changes."

Following Segers's remarks, Neuhaus asked Arons, "Could you respond specifically on the possibility of reconstruction?"

"Remember the end of the period of bureaucracy in the early 1690s," said Arons, "in which there was a kind of desperate refusal to recognize the changing values of the community. That refusal found its expression in an extraordinarily repressive set of trials in which people were accused of being witches and executed. It's that kind of repressiveness that I'm trying to point out."

"Do you see that at work in our society, or at least potentially threatening?" asked Neuhaus.

"Oh yes," Arons replied. "For example, I see what's been characterized as the Religious Right advocating what amounts to a repressive return to the past primarily in order to preserve values which are important, but also as a way of refusing to recognize that something different may be growing."

"With respect to what policy specifics would you see that?" asked Neuhaus.

"I would probably draw most from claims with regard to schooling," answered Arons. "I guess I have to state at the outset here that I have been a defender of the fundamentalist's right to make various changes in the way that schools are operated."

"So you're a proponent of vouchers and alternatives in education," said Neuhaus. "How is the Religious Right being repressive in that? They're simply saying they want greater freedom."

"I make a distinction," Arons countered, "between the Tennessee case, in which people want out for themselves, and the Alabama case, in which people don't want anyone to be able to read the books in question."

A Dangerous Trend

At this juncture, Bradley shifted the focus of the discussion back to Hafen's paper. "I want to respond to Professor Hafen on a couple of things. I'm trying to understand what he senses as the current state of government policy toward mediating institutions, particularly the family. He seems to me to take an excessively benign view, assuming that the authorities, by and large, intervene only to prevent serious harm or serious conflict with key government policies. But it puts me in mind of a certain abortion case. The ruling was extraordinary in the sense that it opened the way for judicial intervention in an ongoing family matter. The situation involved a minor who wanted an abortion, though her parents didn't want her to have it. The court decided the case on the basis of best interest. Ordinarily the legal standard is that you have to show serious harm, not just best interest. Best interest is a standard when there are two parents litigating for a child custody. In any event, I believe that Justice Powell should have said that the child could go to a court and show she would be seriously harmed if she didn't get the abortion, but he didn't do that. He didn't even act as though this was a significant problem."

Pastor Neuhaus asked, "Would you have been happier if he had said that they could intervene because the child had been denied a right to have an abortion?"

"Well, I think that would have been the same thing," Bradley replied. "I'm wondering if Professor Hafen feels that Justice Powell's casual attitude in the institution of that best-interest test was atypical and bizarre, that it is not likely to be the wave of the future. Or is government now more likely to intervene whenever it has a different judgment of the best interest than the parents do? Is this something we should worry about beyond the abortion issue?"

At this point, Hafen responded to several of the participants' comments and questions. "Professor Bradley, it seems to me that a family and a school have more in common with one another than either of them has in common with any other social institution, which is one reason I think the school can be seen as a mediating structure. They are both involved in educating children toward rationality, and that is a unique enterprise. It is long-lasting. It's not an occasional state intervention, and it is vast in its implications. So one of the amusing things I've seen in the court's response to the issue of rationality from children can be illustrated by comparing the whole Establishment Clause line of cases with the free-speech cases involving such things as high school newspapers. For instance, the lower courts have just picked this up all over the place. The most recent example I know of is the case out of the Eighth Circuit that the Supreme Court will hear this fall, in which the high school principal wouldn't allow a couple of stories to be published in the paper. He thought they invaded the privacy of some families and were in other ways unwise and in bad taste. But the court, the Eighth Circuit, reached the conclusion that this was a public forum because in the first issue each year the school paper has in small print a statement that this paper does not represent the views of the faculty and the administration. Or, thinking of *Stone vs. Graham*, the Ten Commandments case, I wondered if it would be possible to have the Ten Commandments on the walls of the schools if at the bottom there were a similar disclaimer—for example, 'The faculty aren't in agreement over these commandments.' Or, 'Some of them like commandments one, four, and nine.' It's a very odd contradiction to me that you can't pray in a school, but you can pray in a legislature. Why? Because the children lack the rational capacity to evaluate who's sponsoring this? But if it's a newspaper, if it's free expression of other kinds, nobody's been concerned about that at all. I don't understand why not.

"Referring to the question of what a family is and whether a family has legal significance, I think family is defined as a legal construct. Why is it that there can be a wrongful death action only when there's been harm to a family relationship? Isn't it odd that there can't be a wrongful death action when you lose your best friend? What interest is there? The countertrend that I mentioned in the essay, that remarkable stability, is still there because the courts won't respond to all the demands about individual rights. I think some of it is linked to concepts about private property and democracy even though the nature of property has changed. There's a sense about the private sphere that's reflected in the legal responsibilities and rights families have. The same thing holds in tax laws, attitudes about immunity from testimony on confidential matters, and things of that kind.

"Let me say just a bit about Bellotti—this is the case involving the pregnant minor who wants an abortion. Massachusetts passed a law requiring parental consent under certain conditions. The court held that the minor girl is entitled to a judicial hearing. At the hearing the judge is to determine if she is mature enough to decide for herself about having the abortion. The court invented a mature minor rule which was cited in a brief from the Attorney General's office in Massachusetts and which had never existed anywhere until it turned up in that brief. There are exceptions on parental consent for minors, but they've always been related to emergencies and such. But never to maturity. So it's a very interesting development. If the judge decides she's not mature, then he decides whether the abortion is in her best interest.

"Finally, I'd be curious to hear a response from someone about the broader issue of the growth of the formal law and its relationship to communal custom. I hypothesize that there's probably some optimal relationship. One of the nice things I've read on that was something Bob Bork wrote a few years ago. It may be more general and abstract than what we've been dealing with, and yet it's very responsive to the basic theme of the conference."

The Final Issues

At this point Neuhaus made some suggestions about the sorts of things the conferees might want to take up in the final session. "I think we're at the right point on this question of the perceived dramatic divergence between formal and customary law. This is putting it in different language, but it's where we were when we began talking about communities of discourse and the divergence between moral discourse and legal discourse which is tied to the whole mediating-structures proposition. The mediating structures are critical because they are the primary—not the only, but the primary—generators and bearers of meaning in a society where people are free to engage one another in rational deliberation about how we ought to order our life together, the political question. So, is the divergence as dramatic and dangerous as some would suggest? How is it related to this question of mediating structures and their not being sustained by legal discourse?

"I think it beyond reasonable doubt to say there is no issue being publicly debated in America that more clearly and painfully joins questions of legal discourse, legal judgment, moral discourse, moral judgment, and disagreements on both sides than the abortion question. In the current issue of the *New Republic*, there is what I consider a very interesting essay, basically flawed but very interesting, by someone who I admire a great deal, Charles Krauthammer. He takes up the whole set of questions on the Baby M case and then goes on to the question of genetic engineering and the use of fetal tissue for neurological purposes. He asks how we are going to deal with these issues, which touch on those surrounding the abortion debate. The abortion debate, he says, and I think rightly, is not a debate over when life begins first of all; rather, it is a debate over what kind of community we're going to be.

"We must find some way of bringing moral and legal discourse back into relationship. We are now faced with a legal-technological set of developments that support the interests of the full-bodied and able-bodied and powerful in our society. In a society like ours, what on earth can prevent the powerful from taking advantage of any and all logical possibilities unless someone can with legal force join moral argument to public effect? How does a particular people stand over against a community that permits anything that is technologically possible?

"In our last session, I would be interested in talking about being the kind of community that can take responsibility not simply for standing over against this awesome and horrendous prospect but for actually attempting in some significant way to prevent the very real possibility that is before us. This means, I think, somehow reconstituting those communities of moral discourse and giving them legal effect."

Berman took up this challenge as he opened the discussion. "We have been talking about mediating structures—such informal or less formal communities as the family, the church, and the schools. I think one should add the neighborhoods, which are also threatened very seriously, and, to some extent, the professions. The threat to these communities is being felt not only in the United States but throughout the industrialized world. The nation is also a community of law and discourse, but the dreadful weakening of the stability of the smaller and more informal communities that constitute the nation has shifted a heavier burden in all the major industrial countries to the state, to the central political authority, producing an enormous problem. At this point the question of formal law comes into view. Customary law has now influenced the formal law. The customary law—the reciprocal, voluntary relationships among people in families, in neighborhoods, and so forth—has developed along lines which we now deplore, with a strong emphasis on individualism and egocentrism, on satisfaction of wants, on the loss of roots and history. As we've been talking about the role of law, we've been thinking mostly about formal law—official law, enacted law, the written law used by the judiciary or the legislature.

"Could law help to reconstruct, reconstitute, and order our lives together in the family, in the community? Here the distinction between customary law and formal law doesn't move us forward; in a sense it moves us backward. We have to reconstitute the customs somehow. It would be futile, it seems to me, for the formal law to attempt simply to reverse this. This is what Bob Bork has suggested. So we have to rebuild, I would think, the customary social relationships that exist.

"What I'm suggesting is that if we're talking seriously about moral discourse, about the role of law and the relation of moral discourse to legal discourse, we should also be talking about the disintegration of the family and the like on the level of the communities in which we exist. This is where the discourse, the combination of legal and moral discourse, has to begin. Our customary law has broken down, and we need discourse also about customary law. There the courts can play a role on all levels and in the matter of all decisions: not just family matters and matters of abortion, but on all levels—commercial matters, property matters, contract matters, and so forth. The courts and our law system have an enormous educational role to play. We should begin to think about law in terms of its persuasive, and not merely its coercive, power."

Professor Buzzard had this to say: "There was some discussion about the relationship of law to the crisis in the family. I think everyone agreed that we're not dealing with law alone, and that perhaps in the context of the family, law was more reflecting the impact of other factors. But law not only reflects culture, it also creates culture. We've seen how *Brown vs. Board of Education* changed a lot of fundamental attitudes—for good or for ill, depending on your point of view. In any case, it suggests to me that when there is an injustice to be redressed, it is a cultural task, not primarily a legal task. If we got ourselves in trouble over a fifty- or one hundred-year span, perhaps we ought to have a long-term strategy to try to redress that. I don't think that the problem is a matter of one or two Supreme Court decisions or a little misunderstanding here or there. We may, in fact, be dealing with problems on the scale of entire worldviews. If we are, that's an enormous agenda that we haven't really begun to address."

Neuhaus added, "It's part of our creed that law is part of

politics and politics is part of culture and the heart of culture is religion. So I agree wholeheartedly with your proposition."

The Monsignor That Was

Father Burtchaell joined the discussion with a confession: "I had a terrible and sinful thought when Richard was giving his unique restatement of where we have come in our discussion. I had an image in my mind that had we been talking about the autonomy of the states and George Wallace had been summarizing the sad state of affairs, it might have sounded just a little bit like some of the problems that we've been discussing about the intrusion of formal law into the mediating institutions. This is not going to be yet another rebel speech, but I am struck by the parallel.

"What were the reasons and what are the occasions for the ascendancy of formal law and the decline of customary consensus that Professor Hafen points out? Well, first of all, there is the decline of authority in mediating communities. Now, it seems to me that in so many of the mediating institutions, communities, and structures a vacuum has been created. There has always been child abuse, but previously there were other people in the family to whom one could appeal who could do something about it. The estrangement, the isolation of the one household was not nearly what it has become today. Sure, there were men kicking their wives down the stairs, but there was also the monsignor who would come when called. I remember cases where that happened and the monsignor would go to the home and give holy hell to the father, threaten him with things that sounded a lot worse than Rikers Island. It was one mediating institution interacting with another. I think it is when people face a general breakdown of many kinds of authority that they appeal in desperation to the agencies of the state, to the police power, to the various forms of relief that the law might attempt to give. But the formal laws of the state can't operate within the family. The state is unable to solve family problems in the family way, the way the monsignor or the grandparent used to do it.

"What's the second reason that the formal law has come to replace what's called the customary law? Well, state sponsorship by the funding of many institutions has brought the queen with her shilling. Think of the different institutions that have been changed by government subsidies. In this way the state has exercised a great estranging power. The growth of federal power has affected mediating institutions in very much the same way it has affected the states.

"I think we might begin our search for a remedy by considering the difference between state management of universities and state management of schools. There are no trustees for schools. Even school boards are in many places heavily compromised. But for universities, even though they are totally funded by the state, there is a board of trustees which in many cases is given real educational, programmatic discretion. I note that this happens whenever the state funds things that have to do with the mind: they tend to look for some sort of clutch, some intermediating transmission that allows money to flow without ideological control. Could we use the same sort of device to restore the autonomy of mediating institutions even when they are subsidized because of their general welfare services?"

Legality and Legitimacy

Following Burtchaell's remarks, Professor Mary Ann Glendon sounded a note of skepticism about the negative consequences of current legal trends on the family. "I'm going to join the people who are doubtful that, insofar as the family is concerned, the law has played a very great role in producing the problem that we all seem to agree exists. I think that family relations are in general resilient and that family law has tended to be preceded and produced by changes in society and the economy more than the other way around. Having said that, I will also say that I think the rhetoric of family law is terribly important. How we characterize things has a modest but not trivial effect on the way we think about and behave with respect to family matters. We have to pay attention to the rhetoric.

"The questions of what a family is and whether there is any legal entity called the family came up earlier. I think it's important to recognize that this legal characterization of the family is a battleground. What is going to be called family is very importantly at stake not only in the United States but elsewhere. Families, after all, are prelegal institutions from the point of view of sociologists and anthropologists. I think it's rather standard in sociological writings to say that marriage is not determinative of whether there is a family. The presence of more than one generation is determinative. So there is always a discrepancy between the social definition of family and the legal definition of family.

"And then it's interesting to consider where the legal definition comes from and how the family is imagined in legal language. That may be the single most dramatic change that has taken place in family law all over the world in developed countries since the 1960s—the shift of definition of family from that founded on marriage, the so-called legitimate family, to de facto family. All over the world the term 'illegitimate children' is suddenly gone.

"So we have to think about the relationship between legitimacy and legality. They are not the same thing. There are some societies in which law is the principal agent in conferring legitimacy. There are other societies in which law does not necessarily control legitimacy. I'm thinking of Ireland, which I visited in December, where great debates are going on about divorce and abortion. But virtually nobody in Ireland thinks of law as the principal indicator of legitimacy. Law is a crooked thing, a foreign thing, an imposed thing, not the main source to which we're going to look for what's right and wrong. I think it is otherwise in the United States, for reasons we've already discussed. We do tend to derive a great deal of our notions of legitimacy from legality. It's very important in our discussions of what a family is to determine whether same-sex couples are going to be called families, for example, because legal definition bestows legitimacy.

"Another example is no-fault divorce. Curious that the United States is the only country in which that particular kind of divorce, which is granted without having to show that the other spouse committed certain kinds of marital wrongs, came to be known as no-fault divorce. By the way, the origin of that is interesting. It migrated into divorce law from tort law, where everybody understands that when you have an automobile accident somebody's usually at fault. It came to carry the meaning, which none of the no-fault reformers intended, that when a marriage breaks up nobody is to blame. And then we go on in our extreme American way to join no-fault with no responsibility for the casualties of divorce."

Walter Berns also sounded a note of skepticism about law's

harm to the family. "I simply want to make the point that the condition of the family is not caused so much by the intervention of the law as by a reduction in the extent to which law protects that community. Years ago the law offered more protection from the vulgarity of the larger world when it intervened in that institution. I'm thinking of such things as censorship. How do parents protect their children from the vulgarity that surrounds us today? How do you protect the cohesiveness of the family from this world we live in? The law used to erect barriers against the corrosive environment of the world, but it no longer does that. It took those barriers down—and look at what has happened."

Arons made a few recommendations about law as a factor contributing to community building. "I want to make two modest suggestions. As I understand it, the mediating structures and the law both function in an underlying role, and I think Lynn Buzzard was quite correct when she said that that is really the central issue. Our only other commonly accepted underlying model is the managerial one, which doesn't confer meaning on people's activities but simply serves to keep them from coming apart at the seams. I think it's necessary to be extremely modest in the kinds of things that we might suggest could be done either by law or by mediating structures to deal with the issue of community building and increasing the moral discourse.

"Two things come to mind. First, we might use the law to strengthen the mediating structures when we are given a chance to do so. But we have to think of doing that in a pluralistic form and in a way that increases rather than decreases participation if we're to get any meaning out of it. My sense from the very last few pages of Professor Hafen's paper was that he wouldn't agree with this. My sense is that we're not so sure that we're willing to tolerate a pluralism of mediating structures. I think that is extremely problematic and is something we should think about very carefully.

"Second, we might use the law not only to strengthen these mediating structures but also to try to reduce the level of formalism within the legal system itself, to demystify and deprofessionalize it to some degree. This is essentially an antilegalist argument. I think that's a necessary condition and a small step to be taken in the direction of making it possible for people to re-create community. My concern in doing such a thing would be that, in the attempt to supplement or augment a moral discourse which I think is pretty much lacking in the law, we not assume that religion is the only legitimate basis for moral reasoning and discourse. I say that with great trepidation, having very graciously been invited to attend this conference in the first place. So just to wrap those two things up, I think that we ought to try to recognize that conflict is useful, that what matters is how we define conflicts and how we resolve them, and that it is necessary to handle conflict pluralistically and antiformalistically.

"As I have reflected on the past two days, some well-known words from Yeats have come into my mind. They are not a reflection on the conference itself but on the problem the conference has been attempting to deal with. I'm referring, of course, to 'The Second Coming': 'the centre cannot hold . . . ;/The best lack all conviction, while the worst/Are full of passionate intensity.'"

"Well let's *hope* that's not a comment on the conference," said Neuhaus.

Reflecting on the discussion during the fourth and last session of the conference, Hafen remarked, "I'd like to say how heartening it has been for me to be here. I'm grateful to have been part of this. I have just two thoughts that grow out of our discussion. One is about schools and churches and families, since we all have interests in those mediating institutions. Part of my worries about the trends that we've been discussing is all the pressure on the people who should exert leadership in mediating structures. All the momentum says that those of us involved in these structures are doing the wrong thing when we try to take seriously our roles of leadership and influence in them. It tells us that when we intervene and try to exercise discretion for the benefit of children or students or members of a church or whatever, that there is somehow something the matter with that. One of my worries about that pressure is that I think it plays into a potentially serious conflict of interest. We're not immune, living in a very affluent society, from the argument that if we would just turn loose all these people who are entitled to such liberation, we would also free ourselves from the responsibility of worrying about them so much. I say that as a reminder, a note of caution that somehow there is a conflict of interest in all the liberation arguments for those of us who try to solve discipline problems in schools or worry about others. It's really a lot easier to quit trying to solve those problems.

"Then, finally, we talked about *duty*—a different word from *rights*, another word we've used a lot. I don't think of duty and liberty as mutually exclusive. I think of them as the poles on a single construct. I don't think that duty has much meaning without reference to liberty and vice versa. Totalitarianism tries to make everything out of duty. Other theories try to make everything out of liberty—anarchy is their best symbol, I think. In my own experience, though, liberty and duty mutually reinforce one another. One is defined in terms of the other. The connection between the two tends to be hidden beneath the surface. We see liberty pop up here, duty there, and they argue with each other. We're misunderstood in talking about duties in communities. But I think our ultimate hope in these conversations is to promote the value of liberty—but a long-term kind of liberty. Seeing the connection between liberty and duty requires a long-term perspective. We need to be patient about that, to refuse to accept short-term solutions, because only in the long run can the two remain linked.

"Let me conclude by echoing one thing from my essay that seemed especially appropriate to me as I wrote in the bicentennial year of the Constitution: the preamble says that we seek to ensure the blessings of liberty not just for ourselves but for our posterity. I am glad to have been in a group that is thinking in a way that encourages me to reach for that. Thank you."

Richard Neuhaus then concluded that "We have deliberated about the process of deliberating about the ordering of our life together, about law and the ordering of our life together. In the process of deliberating, we have in fact done what we have suggested our society needs to do. In that sense it has been, for me, an exemplary conference, and I thank all of you for making it that."

Participants

Frank S. Alexander
School of Law
Emory University

Stephen Arons
Department of Legal Studies
University of Massachusetts

Harold J. Berman
School of Law
Emory University

Walter Berns
American Enterprise Institute
    for Public Policy Research

Robert H. Bork
John M. Olin Sholar in Legal
    Studies
American Enterprise Institute

Gerard V. Bradley
College of Law
University of Illinois

James T. Burtchaell, C.S.C.
Department of Theology
University of Notre Dame

Lynn Buzzard
School of Law
Campbell University

F. Tayton Dencer
The Rutherford Institute

Charles Emmerich
Center for Church/State Studies
The Law School
DePaul University

Hillel Fradkin
The Bradley Foundation

Edward McGlynn Gaffney, Jr.
Loyola Law School

Mary Ann Glendon
The Law School
Harvard University

Martin P. Golding
The School of Law and the
    Department of Philosophy
Duke University

Bruce C. Hafen
J. Reuben Clark Law School
Brigham Young University

Sanford N. Katz
The Law School
Boston College

Douglas W. Kmiec
Office of Legal Counsel
U.S. Department of Justice

Richard John Neuhaus
New York City

Edwin A. Rodriguez
John F. Kennedy School of
    Government
Harvard University

Mary C. Segers
Department of Political Science
Rutgers University